THE
CENTURY
SPEAKS

voices of
WALES

'Old Mary', a centurian from Clun. (Courtesy of the National Library of Wales)

THE
CENTURY
SPEAKS

voices of
WALES

Memories of Welsh people
compiled by Herbert Williams from interviews by Kerry McGeever and Anita Morgan
for the **BBC Radio Wales** *series*
The Century Speaks

TEMPUS

First published 1999
Copyright © BBC Radio Wales, 1999

Tempus Publishing Limited
The Mill, Brimscombe Port,
Stroud, Gloucestershire, GL5 2QG

ISBN 0 7524 1840 8

Typesetting and origination by
Tempus Publishing Limited
Printed in Great Britain by
Midway Clark Printing, Wiltshire

Also by Herbert Williams:

Poetry:
Too Wet for the Devil
The Dinosaurs
A Lethal Kind of Love
The Trophy
Ghost Country
Looking Through Time

Fiction:
A Severe Case of Dandruff (novel)
The Stars in their Courses (short stories)
Stories of King Arthur (for children)

Biography:
John Cowper Powys
Davies the Ocean: Railway King and Coal Tycoon

Other non-fiction:
Come Out Wherever You Are
Stage Coaches in Wales
Railways in Wales
Battles in Wales
The Welsh Quiz Book
The Pembrokeshire Coast National Park
The Mid Glamorgan Book

CONTENTS

Gwen Hughes (nee Jones) with her little sisters Mair (left) and Nan, 1940s. Gwen's reminiscences appear in these pages.

Haymaking in Wales in the early years of the twentieth century. (Courtesy of the National Library of Wales)

FOREWORD

'The Century Speaks' Oral History Project has been one of the biggest tasks ever undertaken by radio broadcasters. During the past year BBC Radio Wales has been doing its part by adding hundreds of voices to an already rich store-house of memories of the century. Welsh people don't need any persuasion to start talking anyway and with the new millennium on the horizon, they've excelled themselves. The gathering of the stories has been a unique experience - the microphone seeming to disappear leaving no barrier between listener and storyteller.

Every part of Wales has been visited and all age groups have been invited to take part in the project. People have shared quite intimate and personal memories of their lives - lots of laughter, some tears (with the interviewers joining in quite often). Join all these threads together and the result is a vivid and rich patchwork quilt of nostalgia mixed with optimism about the coming of the new century.

Writer and broadcaster Herbert Williams was the perfect choice to edit this book to accompany the Radio Wales series because he has the poet's eye, the broadcaster's ear and what's more he comes from Aberystwyth! I hope you will enjoy the words and the pictures that Herbert has chosen to accompany them. This is your chance to find out what the people of Wales have to say about themselves at the end of the twentieth century.

Anita Morgan
Producer/Presenter
BBC Radio Wales

Kerry McGeever
Producer
BBC Radio Wales

A production in 1938 of the operetta Y Blodyn Glas (The Blue Flower) at Gorffwysfa Chapel, Sling, near Bangor. Mrs Hannah Rowlands was the producer and her memories appear in this book.

ACKNOWLEDGEMENTS

Our thanks to all who gave the interviews to the BBC which made this book possible. We are especially grateful to those who generously lent us photographs.

CHAPTER 1

Where we live

'On the cusp of Cardiff' – Andrew and Louise Prynne's house at Culverhouse Cross.

Louise Prynne with her twin daughters Helun and Zoe, then three months old.

Family Network

We live in Culverhouse Cross, on the cusp of Cardiff. In the last few years this has become an out-of-town retail centre so sometimes it's like living in the middle of a department store. It suits us because my partner and I both work and Grandma is just around the corner. It's literally five minutes from the M4 and 10 minutes from the centre of Cardiff.

I had a fairly idyllic upbringing in the small town of Cowbridge, about 12 miles from Cardiff. I don't think we have such a good environment for the children here but I have a good extended family so that compensates. My husband's parents actually live on this development, 200 yards from us, and Great-Grandma lives nearby in Wenvoe village. My father still lives in Cowbridge and so do my sisters, so we have a brilliant network. Sometimes I think, 'Gosh, there's a whole day gone by without seeing any of my family' and I suppose that's unique these days.

Louise Prynne, born 1958

Small and Friendly

I'm fifteen years old. I'm from Rhayader, a small town in mid Wales. It's quiet and friendly and everyone knows your business! I prefer it in the country as it would be rougher in the city and you'd have to watch your back. We live in a bungalow at the top of quite a steep hill, so it's quite cold in the winter. All three bedrooms are small, especially mine. I don't usually clean my room – Mum does that - but if it's a real mess I'll tidy it up. I've got posters – footballers on one wall, music artists on the others – Liam Gallagher, Thom Yorke, people like that. I've got everything I need, TV and videos. Whenever I'm in I just watch videos and listen to music.

James Price, born 1984

Dying Valley

We moved to Tonteg in 1990. It's dying here, isn't it? When I was a kid I done my training for the colliery in Ogmore Vale. That little valley used to have three pits and the place was bubbling. You go up there now, it's dead.

Pontypridd's another place – everything was vibrant, now everything's shut. It's the same everywhere. Llanharry has expanded as a commuter place, there's no industry there now. The iron mine has gone, Llanharry dairy's shut down, the pits are shut down, people have just got to commute. Where they've built them new houses in Llanharry, I'd never buy one because we used to play underneath there in the old drift mine. They must have about 30 feet of cover between them and the great big holes where they worked the iron out years ago.

Dai Lawrence, born 1942

Lucky To Be Here!

This is actually my parents' house but when I think of a house I think of here. It's an old Welsh farmhouse which was extended in the nineteenth and early twentieth centuries, and the holiday cottages which surround it were once farm cottages and barns and an old stable, so it's just been developed over the years. I'm here now with my children and it comes back to me how wonderful and lucky I've been to have grown up in a house like this. You can see out to Snowdon and you can see the sea at Cricieth and the golf course is just behind us. My grandmother used to live in this house. My parents had the house next door and my father farmed the land. My brother then took over the farm and turned the sheep shed into a house for himself and his family. It's literally only 20 yards away so we're all in this little circle of buildings. There's eleven of us living here in total but

we've got enough space, which is great. I got married in 1991 and we went to live out in Spain. Basically I went there to live with my husband and we bought a house, but then unfortunately he left. We've come back for obvious reasons, it's for the children, it's for stability. They know the house and the oldest one goes to a local school in Cricieth, but we're going to move to Llanfair PG and start afresh.

Davina Carey-Evans, born 1965

You Could Drop Dead in the Street ...

I was born sixty-four years ago in Tremorfa in Cardiff, and that's where I

Danielle Crane, aged ten – Queen of the Menai Straits, 1999.

Daisy Evans – 'Thanks, you saved my life!'

still live. My father was a baker and my mother a caterer, and I was a steelworker. I'm retired now. I've lived in London and various other places, but moved back to Cardiff when my parents became elderly. The area has changed horrendously. The old neighbourliness has gone. There was no house I couldn't go into as a child. You could even have a meal or sleep at your friend's house. In my house children were bathed and put to bed with me and that wasn't unusual. It was a very close community – you could spot a stranger coming in, it was that close, and it was a very caring community. The old people and very badly disabled people lived amongst us without any help from the Social Service or whatever. People were looked after by their children or parents, there was no problem. If Mrs So-and-So was taken ill you just took the children into the house. It didn't seem like you were doing a social service, it was just accepted. But now you could drop dead in the street and they'd walk over you.

Graham Willis, born 1935

Something to Leave the Kids

I only ever lived in one house when I was growing up – a three-bedroom council house in Bangor. There were my twin brothers and myself and my sister and obviously Mam and Dad. I slept in one bedroom with my twin brothers and my sister had a little bedroom. The twins had bunk beds at first but as they grew older they had separate single beds, so then the room was really packed! They're six years older than me. Mam and Dad rented the house off the council – they still do. I've tried to explain to them that with all the rent they've paid they could have bought the house twice over but no, they're not bothered. The council estate was very rough – it's one of the largest estates in North Wales. I was lucky, I had two elder brothers, and if someone picked on you, you'd just tell your big brother and he'd sort them out. It wasn't so bad when they were younger – it all changed in the mid to late '70s. That's when it started getting really bad. You used to get fights between the top and bottom parts of the estate on bonfire night. Awful. I've bought my own home now in Menai Bridge. I wanted something to leave for the kids as I got older. We've got two girls, aged ten and two.

Michael Crane, born 1966

The Middle of Nowhere

I live sort of in the middle of nowhere. There's a lot of animals around and my house used to be a farm. I used to live in Cardiff but I prefer living here as I used to have asthma in Severn Grove and it's absolutely gone now. The air is much cleaner.

The house is big. It's a bit tattered so we're starting to do it up. My bedroom's lovely though, it's very big with a bed and an inflatable chair – I got that for Christmas. I've got a radio in my bedroom of my own. Mum's got one in their bedroom and there's one downstairs in the kitchen so we've got a lot of radios. We've got a computer – that's what the boys play on, Elis and my half-brother Joshua – he's older

than me. Elis does his thank-you letters on the computer, he finished them a month ago. There's always a reason not to do them. Mum told me to do them and then you just came in – thanks, you saved my life!

Daisy Evans, born 1990

Community Spirit

I come from the village of Abercwmboi but after we got married we came to live in Cwmaman. It's a dead-end village – you actually can't drive out the other end – so because of that it's very much retained its community presence. The Miners'

Tyrone O'Sullivan.

Welfare is still the centre of what goes on there – of course it's a drinking club now – the brass band meet there, the choir, the operatic society, the Labour Party, Plaid Cymru, and I'm very lucky to be in a community that's so supportive. We've even built our own outdoor swimming pool.

Tyrone O'Sullivan, born 1946

New Ways of Living

We're living in a first-floor flat in a converted barn in Pembrokeshire. It was the old granary in a farm courtyard. We've got a wood-burning stove in the middle of a large room which heats the whole space. It's a small community here and we've tried to make the individual homes and spaces as compact and energy-efficient as possible. There are four families with children – altogether there are thirteen adults and eleven children at the moment. We all have our own private spaces and we also have shared communal spaces in the big farmhouse. We eat communally four or five nights a week and take it in turns to cook for each other. We have one day a week when we work all together and then we work at different things at other times. We have meetings to discuss the affairs of the community and we share the work on the land. I'm a musician and I also make baskets. I like spinning and weaving and I've been one of the main gardeners here – I grow all the vegetables and fruit, and I milk the goats and take part in all the general work on the farm. We've got 60 acres of woodland and are completely self-sufficient. We also generate our own electricity from the stream and we have a windmill and solar water heating. I think humans have to learn to change and find ways of living which don't harm the earth so we describe ourselves as a site for experimental sustainable living.

Emma Orbach, born 1954

Panoramic Views

My father saw something special about this cottage. He opened up this mountain really. He didn't cut the hedge down, I did that and then the views came along, panoramic views. Caldy Island on a fine day, Worms Head

Ray Gravell.

14

in Gower, the Gwendraeth Fach – the area is steeped in history. I look down on Kidwelly Castle and that's important because there's still a feeling of 'them' and 'us.' Some mornings all I can see is the castle turret sticking up through the mist and the church steeple and it's quite mesmeric. I can well understand how the people of the Middle Ages believed what they believed in then. It's quite magical, very mystical and so appealing. Time stops for me. There's no day, no hour, just now.

What my father found here was a certain freedom. Mynydd y Garreg – the Mountain of Stone – is directly behind us. He was a coal miner. He loved the garden, shooting rabbits and ferreting. He taught me all those things as a little boy. His great joy was to go on the mountain.

Ray Gravell, born 1952

I'm Not So Soft Now

When we moved into this farmhouse we had two carpets and two chairs and a bed and not a pair of curtains. We didn't bother at all. We've been very lucky – we've been given things by both sides of the family. I hate anything looking new.

William's family have always been in farming but I was brought up in Birkenhead. I was quite soft when I came here but you harden quite rapidly. I had a pet, the first lambing – I looked after this little lamb and it died and I cried and cried. And now I just go round the dead lambs and put them in bags, you know? It's funny how you become like that. It's not cruel, you just become realistic. That's the difference between city people and country people – this great divide. They've humanised animals – that's how I used to be too. I

Gwredog Farm, where William and Jenny Edwards live in Rhosgoch, Anglesey.

think everybody should go on a farm for a few months, especially at lambing time, then they'd have a good idea of what things are like.

Jenny Edwards, born 1953

I Couldn't Sleep for the Quiet!

We're living now outside Resolven. It was one of the busiest roads in Wales at one time but in the last couple of years there's been a new road up the valley so we've seen a vast difference. The children couldn't go out on the pavement before for fear of getting knocked down but now they've

Farmer's wife Jenny Edwards with her son David, then seven – smiling bravely although hurt after falling off a bale of hay – and daughter Claire, five. On the left is a family friend, Elizabeth Cemlyn-Jones.

certainly improved the environment. In fact, after the new road was built I couldn't sleep for two or three nights because everything was so peaceful.

Graham Harris, born 1960

Planting Trees for Posterity

This [Cefn Tilla Court, Usk] is a fifteen-bedroom house originally built in 1616, added to greatly in 1858 and given to my great-great-grandfather by 1,700 friends or thereabouts by public subscription at that date. It's in the middle of the country with few buildings in sight, a nice garden and two additions, one a Jacobean square and the other a Victorian addition that goes on and on. It's very cleverly designed really in what they used to call a 'virage', where you go through an area and suddenly there's another with a different view and you go on like that indefinitely. I quite enjoy gardening – I like the effect rather than the actual labour. I'm very good with the weed-killer … The drive has got into the most terrible tangle so I took the opportunity of having some trees felled – a lot of rubbishy timber really – and I've planted it up with some nice ornamental trees, which should have been done fifty years ago and wasn't. I've just planted an avenue of red oak, sixty so far, and there'll probably be enough for my next birthday, my seventy-third – one for every year of my life. They'll take several hundred years to mature. The textbooks say some will grow to six feet in diameter but I shan't be around then. They say that when old men plant trees it's a wish to be

Graham Harris on his horse Trigger at Resolven gymkhana, 1973.

remembered. I sleep in the room where I was born – that's not very usual, is it? I used to go to the House of Lords quite a lot, and I had a flat in various places – Earls Court, Chelsea, Regents Park. I've moved around and I love London, yes. I'm pegged here by the way I was born but if I were deprived of it I think I'd be quite happy to live in London.

Lord Raglan, born 1927

Closer Links Now

I'm very much a townie, born and bred in Llanelli. I'm tempted very often to go into the rural parts of Wales to live but the prices are far too high. I think the link between townies and people who live in the countryside is much

closer now than it's ever been, because country people come to town and town people go to the country. There's a greater understanding of the people who live in rural areas – for example, in a recession they're the first to experience hardship and the last to have the benefits that come from an upturn in the economy.

David Morris, born 1931

Friends for Life

Up to the age of three I was brought up in a council house in the little village of Parcllyn, just north of Cardigan, and then my parents built a new home in the village of Aberporth. We moved there when I was four and

One of the last trains to run through Resolven, in the Neath Valley.

Winter on Gwredog Farm, Rhosgoch.

lived there till I was 14, when my parents moved back to their childhood home in Bethesda, near Bangor. I am very much a country person. Parcllyn and Aberporth were country areas and the same goes for this part of north Wales. Certainly Aberporth was a farming area and most of my friends lived on farms. One of the main differences between farmers and town people is the very close and friendly relationships you build up over a period of time. You don't get to know them at once – they're not all upfront. It takes months or even years to work at the relationship, but once you've made friends with them farming families are friends for life. They're also people with a long folk memory, if I can put it that way, they remember family history or local history; they are fascinating people to be with and talk to.

I think town people seem to have very little sympathy with the country areas and show little understanding of what tending the land actually means. They see farming as quite a romantic occupation but in fact it's the economic life blood of many parts of Wales. I don't think they always have respect for people who make their living in the countryside. They don't understand the craft of looking after animals and managing the land, and I think there's a feeling as well that the country is largely a recreational area, if you like, something to play in and enjoy and not really respected and looked after as it should be.

Dafydd Roberts, born 1956

Alfred Lawes.

The Mountains of Maerdy

It's the last place I'd want to live in – a city. I look out the window here in Maerdy and see the mountains. I was brought up in the mountains and when I die I'll be buried beneath the mountains and that's it.

Alfred Lawes, born 1919

CHAPTER 2
Childhood

Sally David with her sister Louise.

Cowboys and Indians

I live about three and a half miles from my childhood home in Welshpool. If I stand at the window I can see it. I remember that as a place of extreme hardship. My brother and sisters have rosier memories because they left at sixteen. I remember no electricity, very bad winters, carrying bags of food, sacks of flour, being snowed in for weeks at a time and having to dig our way out. But at the same time it was very beautiful in the summer. We were a very happy community. Everybody knew everybody else and nobody had much so we shared a lot. Children played together but we didn't go in each other's houses. We knew the limits and we knew exactly whose fields we could go in and whose we couldn't. My parents were wonderful. They were very strict, my mother particularly so. My father was a figure that came home and was always gentle. He used to say, 'Mummy tells me you've been naughty and I'm supposed to smack you but …' My father was a Londoner so he had a different way with him. I remember a lot of hardship and a lot of laughter and we all had wonderful chances. We lived beneath a wood so the wood became our playground. We played cowboys and Indians – it was magic. We had an old car we used to drive round the wood without brakes, but our Dad didn't know this until he said he'd put new brakes on and then he had to know. We used to swing and climb - we were very athletic.

Sally Pryce, born 1945

There Was Always Singing

I always remember the sink, or the bosh as we used to call it, by the side of the back door, no hot water just that, and right opposite was the old-fashioned pantry with the stone shelf which kept everything cold, and it seemed very often that the house was always cold except for the metre or two around the fire. I was part of the street and we all knew each other. My father worked in the coal mine here (Tower Colliery) and he was a very keen gardener. He also had a dog and kept pigeons. He wouldn't change napkins, he wouldn't iron, you wouldn't see him with a sweeping brush but he was very caring and also very macho.

My mother looked after myself, my brother and sister and I think we were spoilt in many ways. One thing we had to do was the shopping, whether we were in school or not. My auntie owned the shop so it wasn't too bad. The shop has been there now 50 years. My mother was always soft and tender. Mind, she used to lose her temper and lock my brother and myself in the outside toilet if we really misbehaved, and that was quite an experience because it was always dark. My father was very gentle but strict in lots of ways. He was killed here at Tower Colliery when I was seventeen. It's hard to assess now looking back, but he was more of a friend and a brother. He used to play with us, cricket and football and tennis. He was very active in that way. My mother was a singer with the local operatic society so she was always singing around the house. My Auntie Kath used to sing about Rose Marie, she really believed she was Jeanette

McDonald. My father was like an uncle to the street, that was the kind of warmth he created.

Tyrone O'Sullivan, born 1946

Tea on the Table

I was brought up in a really traditional home in Cowbridge, in the Vale of Glamorgan. I'm one of three girls and Mum was home all the time. My father was able to come home for lunch as he had his butcher's shop not far away. Mum had lunch ready on the table for him and when we came home tea was ready. We knew most of the shopkeepers – John the Ironmonger and Glyn the Boot and the rest. It was a really good community to grow up in. We used to camp in the fields behind the house and one day we even had electricity in the tent – we were totally indulged children. We weren't allowed to play with other kids on a Sunday – it was a family day, with Sunday lunch. My Mum wouldn't have considered going shopping on a Sunday and look what happens now. I still think it's good to sit down as a family at the table for Sunday lunch but we don't often do it now. The big problem is that you don't finish till three and all you want to do then is sleep, so the day has gone.

Louise Prynne, born 1958

Left: Dad came home for lunch as his shop wasn't far away. *Right:* Herbert David at his butcher's shop in Cowbridge.

All Sorts of Mischief

I was brought up in Bontgoch, in north Cardiganshire. I was born in 1915 and went to Bontgoch Church of England School. We were taught mostly in English, although it was only Welsh at home. I couldn't speak a word of English when we started school. The headmaster was Rhys Jones, an ex-army man. He'd been an officer in the First World War, serving in Ireland. He had a big cane in his desk so he used to thrash us, no half measures. You had to hold your hand out and get a few slaps. We were afraid of him, you know. My mother was from Llanbrynmair but she died when I was about six years old, of TB. She was only a young woman – I can't remember much about her. We were three girls and myself. My father was a farmer with 300 acres, mainly cattle and sheep. After my mother died I remember an old lady looking after us, Mrs Hughes from Aberystwyth. She was the housekeeper.

The tramps stayed the night in the workhouse in Aberystwyth, then they'd go on to Machynlleth. They'd get a meal in the workhouse and be turned out the next day.

We had plenty of freedom – too much, I suppose. Up to all sorts of mischief. I remember going around crows' nests with a friend of mine and stealing their eggs – Duw, Duw . We used to go fishing and shooting – hares, rabbits, crows. I had a gun when I was fourteen.

Dewi Evans, born 1915

Dr Emyr Jones and his wife Phyllis at Quarry Hospital, Bethesda, in 1931.

Monkey Business

My father was a hospital doctor who looked after hundreds of quarrymen in Bethesda. Some of the men would die and I always remember my mother saying, 'I hope he said goodbye to his wife in a friendly way this morning.' All my life I've never let the children or anybody leave the house without making up, whatever the circumstances. It was a big, big house. Mam kept hens and used to take them to shows – she had peacocks too. It was an amazing period of my life. Later my father became a GP in Penrhyndeudraeth. Taid (Grandfather) was a character. He was a sea captain on

Four-year-old Gwen Jones with her Taid (grandfather), Capt. William Pritchard.

oil tankers and drove his Austin 16 right in the middle of the road, as if it was a tanker! I think he was the greatest menace in the village. He brought a black boy home from sea with him on one occasion. Well, you can imagine, in those days there were all kinds of funny remarks and people wanted to touch him to see if the black came off his face. Another time he brought a monkey home. A lady came to tea one day with a smart hat with cherries on it. She went to the outside toilet and was a long time coming back because the monkey had followed her and was poking his paws through the door trying to pinch the cherries!

Auntie Maggie used to make butter in an electric churn, a huge wooden thing. She put the butter in a mould which had a picture of a cow on it. I'd walk miles and miles to see Uncle John – I idolised him. He was a strapping big man and I'd go fishing in the lakes with him and potter around, picking bilberries or whatever.

Gwen Hughes, born 1933

Killing the Pig

It was two up and two down where we lived in William Street, Llanelli. The lavatory was at the top of the garden next to the pig sty. We bathed every Friday in the zinc bath. My father, who was a collier, bathed every day in front of the fire. The fire was a big thing in our house. I think we had a much happier time than children now in spite of the poverty that surrounded our lives. Everybody helped everybody else. For example, we kept a pig and my Uncle George next door kept chickens, so we would kill the pig and

share half the proceeds with him, except you couldn't see my arse for dust when they killed the pig. They would share the eggs or the chicks and we would share the bacon and hams. Everybody kept their peelings for Uncle George. There were six of us in the house. I doubled up with my parents and my step-sister doubled up with my grandparents. Of course we became sexually aware and I was shuffled off downstairs to the front room where there was a bed settee and Glenys occupied the settee in the kitchen. It was glorious because it meant I could stay up very late.

The man I knew as my father left home when I was eleven and my mother married again – Stan Rees, a marvellous man. It was during the time of the divorce that she told me I was her

Phyllis Pritchard – Capt. Pritchard's daughter – smartly dressed in the mode of the time.

adopted child. I'd guessed there was something different about me though I couldn't explain it. Every three or six months a man would come around in a peaked cap and inspect us and I'd be on my best behaviour in my best clothes and I'd have to wash my neck. He'd look at my ears and teeth and clothes. He was a child inspector and because I was adopted he came to make certain I was safe and well. I'd been brought from Kidderminster when I was six weeks old. I've discovered since that I've got two brothers and four sisters, all living in Tenby and Manorbier. It was clear that my mother and so-called grandparents loved me very much. I waited until my adoptive mother died before doing anything because I didn't want to hurt her. When she passed away I started making tentative enquiries and found that my natural mother was Augusta (Gussie) White. I met her once before she died. When she came to the door, she looked at me and said 'Lawrence.' That in fact was the name of my actual blood father. I looked just like him. I don't know if he's alive today. I heard on the grape vine that he went to Scotland after making Augusta pregnant. She was very lucky that she wasn't declared mentally unstable and put in an institution or workhouse – they could do that in those days. She was seventeen when I was born.

David Morris, born 1931

I Missed My Dad

I missed my father terribly when he went to the army because he used to take me out a lot. He took me for walks in the spring looking for flowers and I remember swimming with him. He always gave a lot of time to me. My younger brother was rather a sickly little boy so my mother had to concentrate a lot of her efforts on him, but my father was always there and did things for me. I can remember the morning he went away, standing screaming, bouncing my feet up and down on the doorstep. When he came back from the Army… he wasn't a tall man, you see … he walked in and I stood up and thought, 'This isn't my father.' He was this sort of slightish man with a great mop of fairish hair bleached white. You see, when he'd gone away to the Army I'd been a little one and he'd seemed big to me, but when he came back I was five foot three or whatever …

Olwen Burton, born 1933

Street Football

I'm from a big family of ten children. One died as a baby in the 1930s but there were seven boys and two girls and mother and father in a three-bedroom house. I remember things like seven boys in a bedroom – three in one bed, two in another and two in another – two sisters in a little box room and my father and mother in the middle-sized bedroom. We all lived in a council house up in Townhill, Swansea, in a street where there was a lot of big families. There were nine or ten children in five or six of the houses and the street was full of children. It was always forty to fifty for football in the street, things like that you know. On Boxing Day married men would play the

Hockey teams in Caernarfon County School and Bethesda County School.

single men in football, or on a weekend the under-30s would play the over-30s. You had a look-out at the top of the street and a look-out at the bottom to watch for the bobbies because you weren't allowed to play football on the street. I remember one Sunday morning a policeman came and everybody ran into the one house. My auntie lived there – well, we called her Auntie Hughes but she wasn't my auntie really, everybody was auntie in those days – we all went into her house and the policeman came to the door and there were blokes up the stairs and in the bedrooms, the living-room was full. Mrs Hughes went to the door and the policeman said, 'They've been playing football' and she said 'No, they're not here.' He knew what was happening but didn't do anything about it like.

Terry Stewart, born 1943

Science was for Boys

My grandmother was the boss of my mother, you know. Children are brought up so differently now. I never remember having a cuddle or a kiss from my mother or my aunties, oh there was no time for that. My aunties always told me off and so did my grandmother. I remember one thing though – I sometimes cry when I say this – my mother wanted a new dress but when she found I'd failed history at Bethesda school she bought me a mac and a pair of shoes with the money she'd saved up for the dress. So you see kissing was nothing, was it? My father was a quarryman and my brother and I were in the county school. My brother went to

university but the teacher stopped me doing science. I was top of my form in maths and we were going to do 'O' levels – Central Welsh Board it was called then, the matric – and she went through the class asking us all what we wanted to do. When I told her she said, 'Yes, Hannah Hughes, you want to do science so that you can be with the boys.' I kept quiet about it, I didn't tell father because I thought he'd believe her and tell me off. So I dropped maths, my best subject, and that's what spoilt me going to the university and everything. I've hated that woman ever since.

Hannah Rowlands, born 1909

I've Disowned My Family

When I was about six or seven my mother and father were always arguing and fighting. It was just me and my brothers that were getting the brunt of it because it was like he [my father] had a lot of problems himself when he was younger. I'll refer to him as Chris and to my mother as Anne. I don't really like to know them as my mother and father but I haven't got a much of a choice because they were the ones that gave birth to me. It was constantly arguing and because Chris couldn't handle it he just said, 'Bugger it, put 'em in care.' I've disowned the majority of my family now, you see, it's been so long I have to think about it. The relationship between Anne and Chris broke down when I was about ten or eleven but I was in care by then. I would say I was an exceptionally difficult child but I'd also say I had a lot

Left to right: Mair Jones (later Mair McGeever), Edith the maid and Mair's sister Nan, in the late 1940s.

of excuse from the way I was brought up. I was put into care because they didn't want me. As I've got older and maturer I've kind of put two and two together. I've got my feet on the ground but my Mum is saying things like 'My long lost son.' I don't want to know because she didn't want to know me when I was a kid so she isn't going to know me now. I see Chris walking in Barry sometimes and he calls over and asks me how I am and I say 'Fine' and just walk on. The last time I spoke to him, flippin' heck it must be about three years ago.

Richard Grant, born 1982

Father was King

My home was a complete haven. I had the most wonderful parents.

We lived in a big terraced house in Caernarfon but when I was four we moved to a detached house at the top of the street. It had three main floors with about eight bedrooms. Edith, our maid, who is incredibly important in our upbringing, came then. I was four, Nan was one and Gwen was eleven. Edith was a complete star. She was like a second mother and she cleaned so the house was always spotless. She shopped and cooked. My mother studied law and she also played golf and had a considerable amount of freedom. I think she did resent a little bit Edith's hold on the whole family but she tried to be glad about it. My father was a doctor who was adored by a lot of people in north Wales. He was a consultant at the C and A Hospital in Bangor and he was royally treated, like a king. He didn't do anything in the house. He had two weaknesses. He had nice cars and he had to smoke. We went to the local school. We all three of us were captain of the hockey team, I think, prefects and all that – very Welsh! We rarely spoke English, and that could be a bit of a nightmare when my parents had English friends to dinner, as we were told we had to speak English and that was hard.

Mair McGeever, born 1940

I Learned to Fight Pretty Quick

I was born in London – Wimbledon, to be precise. My mother's English and my father's Welsh. I was born in the war and lived in my Granny's house in London. I remember the air raid sirens going off and everyone diving down the tin shelter in the garden. My grandfather was a miner

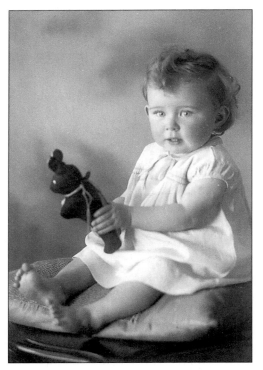

A very young Mair McGeever.

most of his life. He finished up working in the iron ore mine in Llanharry. We came down to live in the area when I was eleven and my life at school was made hell for a few weeks because I spoke different to everyone else. I really sympathise with coloured people moving into a white area. I learned to fight pretty quick – you had to, or God help you. But it all worked out in the end, no problem. I wanted to give my kids a good education so I looked around at the schools and I noticed that the Welsh [language] schools had no graffiti on the walls and the kids were well behaved. In the English schools round here you'd see graffiti everywhere and nobody seemed to care so I sent the kids first of all to a Welsh nursery and then to Welsh primary and secondary schools. Now my eldest boy's in university and the seventeen-year-olds are in college and of course they're all bilingual. The only thing that upset me is, the kids would never speak Welsh at home, always English. If they spoke Welsh I'd pick it up but no … but we muddle through, you know.

Dai Lawrence, born 1942

Rook Pie and Rabbit

We had a staff of six [at Cefn Tilla Court]. There was a housekeeper and a cook – my father never had a butler – a scullery maid and parlour maid and a house maid and a nursery maid. And then there was a nanny and a governess. There were four of us, rather spread out. You needed them because things were much more difficult to keep clean in those days. There was no electricity here until 1951 so there were no Hoovers.

A scene from old Swansea – Nelson Street, at the rear of the Empire Theatre.

Everything got dirty because there were coal fires which made things filthy. One of my earliest memories is of a housemaid opening one of the windows and shaking out dusters in the air. It probably all blew back in again. It was always dusty and because there were lots of poor people around in those days, you were expected to take on a number of staff out of your duty to provide employment. Certainly they didn't get much money but they had good food and lodging. We had one marvellous, lovely cook who came here as a parlourmaid in 1929 and only left in 1964 and I kept up with her, of course, until she died. She kept the whole place together for years and years. Everything revolved around her really. There were lots of rabbits and she was very good with roast rabbit with bacon round it, and rooks in the spring. Young rooks would hop out on the branches. They couldn't fly and one used to shoot them with a

rifle to have rook pie. 'Four and twenty blackbirds baked in a pie' was probably something to do with that! Rook pie was a very common country dish – rooks weren't looked on with great favour because they did a lot of damage in harvest time, when the ground was too hard for them to get their beaks into for insects. They knocked down the harvest so the farmers thinned them out. They tasted strong, but very good.

My mother was a follower of a dietician who was very popular in the '20s and '30s who was against fried foods so we were brought up without them. We weren't allowed fried bacon and very rarely sausages and I never ate a potato chip until I was about 16. I always have chips now as a treat when I go out but I never eat them at home. We had porridge of course and boiled fish, that sort of thing, and no orange squash out of a bottle in those days. Sometimes as a great treat in the summer we had home-made lemonade.

Lord Raglan, born 1927

Wringing Out the Blankets

I was born in the St Thomas district of Swansea and actually went to the school opposite our house. In the early '30s we moved to a local authority house and that was the first time I saw hot and cold taps and a flushing toilet inside. They were referred to as corporation houses in those days and moving in was a luxury. I can remember my father painting the house and everything was done in bottle green. He loved his garden and took tremendous pride in it. My mother was a lovely lady, a hefty lady and very strong. I can remember her washing the clothes out the back in a zinc bath – strong arms,

wringing out the blankets. I could never understand how she could twist the blankets round to look like a python. Of course, in the same boilers they used to boil the puddings for Christmas. She made big Christmas cakes and we took them across for the local baker to bake. Lovely times, lovely times.

Charles Thomas, born 1928

Cavemen of Cardiff!

When I was a boy, the nuns at Nazareth House in Cardiff had their own dairy herd. They were equal to making their own cheese and butter, and some of those women could even repair roofs! The animals used to run through the streets with a herdsman behind them, taking them to the slaughterhouse two miles away. It may raise a few eyebrows

Morris Lane School in the St Thomas district of Swansea, 1933. The young Charles Thomas is second from the right, seated.

No stinting the celebrations in 1936! The scene in Pinkney Street, Swansea, for King George V's jubilee.

today, but it's true. When you come to think of those far-off days before World War One, Cardiff's traffic was mainly horse-drawn – and there'd be donkeys too. There used to be a street called Donkey Street because nearly everybody there had a donkey. They kept it out the garden and went buying and selling scrap iron and blocks of wood. It was a different world altogether. There was no help from the State. You'd see women in the street, with babies close to their breasts, singing 'Alice Blue Gown' or one of the other songs of the day, trying to get a couple of coppers to buy food. And there were the Cave Men of Ely River. About six of them dug a big hole in the banks of the river by the tollgate near the pumphouse in Penarth Road. They reinforced it with corrugated iron sheet and lived in it. They retrieved driftwood from the river and used that for their means of warmth. There was a lot of poverty then. The women didn't know where the next meal was coming from. I

had boys in my class at school with no home, sleeping in the porch of houses after the people had gone to bed, overcoat over them and they would go to school next day. The poverty was really terrible.

William (Bill) O'Neill, born 1908

Rissole Delight

My father did a lot of housework because my mother used to work with the local undertaker until about half-past five. I finished school at 4 o'clock and father came home about twenty-past four. We had good basic food. You never saw Chinese or Indian food years ago. There were two chips shops in Resolven, Ned Chips and Mrs Iles and the highlight of the week would be to have a rissole.

Graham Harris, born 1960

Eleven-year-old Graham Harris at Ynysfach Primary School.

I've Got to be on Wheels

I'm seventy-four and my husband Shadrack (Shady) is two years younger – he's my toy boy! I was born in Monmouth in my parents' caravan and my children were born in a caravan and I hope to die in one because I wouldn't go anywhere else. I've got to be on wheels. I'm the fourth or fifth Rebecca on my father's side – his name was Day.
On washing day you'd have a big line outside and a primus stove to boil the clothes in, an old-fashioned bath and paraffin lamps. When we put the caravan on Caerleon Common the lady in a nearby cottage called us 'my once a year neighbours.'

Rebecca (Becky) Scarrott, born 1925

Fairgrounds

The old fairgrounds had clowns, jesters, pots and pans men. When I was growing up there were all sorts of things - elastic balls, teasers squirting water over the girls, chairoplanes, Noahs Arks ... and the fairgrounds themselves, you look at the old photographs, the women in their hats ... today there's hardly any women wearing hats.

Shadrack (Shady) Scarrott, born 1927

Rat-tat-tat Ginger

I was born in Cyprus and came over here when I was five. It was a corner house with a shop front, a little reception room just where the front door was and another very small TV room and that was it. There was a kitchen and an outside toilet but no bathroom and we bathed in a tin bath. There were three bedrooms upstairs. Later we had an extension downstairs with a new kitchen and an inside toilet and bathroom. That must have been in the late '60s or early '70s. We played out in the streets – I think parents are a bit more worried now about their children running around freely but there wasn't much traffic then. We used to play football in the streets and rat-tat-tat ginger and we'd have running races round the block. We all mucked in like one big family. We used to have tournaments with kids from the next street, oh we had some fun!

Taz Lazarou, born 1955

Adoption was Taboo

I didn't have a sense of identity because I was adopted. I was told at a devastatingly early age – I was just turned three. I'd started going to school and there were several adopted children in the town at the time – it was very fashionable during the Second World War to force unwed mothers to give them up for adoption. It was part of social hygiene – cleaning up the loose ends of society. What happened is that one of my mother's friends who had adopted twins had been traumatised because the twins had been told on the school playground that they were adopted. They hadn't known this and ran home to ask if it was true. One of these little girls had reacted with extreme emotion and rejected her adoptive mother and become what was known then as a maladjusted child. My mother justified explaining to me about my adoption when I was so little because of this experience of her friend. She said she didn't want me to be shocked and it was pretty obvious that she didn't want me to reject her. My mother never spoke to me about the fact of adoption afterwards except on one occasion when I was five, to remind me because she said it seemed as if it hadn't sunk in. Of course the fact hadn't just sunk in, it had absolutely exploded my sense of security and the reason I wasn't talking about it was because it had been made perfectly plain in a thousand and one ways that it was a taboo subject. It was even more taboo than sex. I do think of it as something terribly cruel and insensitive, imposed on little children and in that period handled with utter disdain for the child's sensitivity, intelligence and humanity. The idea was that you could pick up a person by their roots and dump them somewhere else like a sack of potatoes, or let's say the bulb of a tulip – stick it in the earth and it would just grow up as if nothing had happened.

Nerys Patterson, born 1943

Picking up the Socks

My father worked on the farm and went to London quite a lot to NFU meetings and that sort of thing. My mother was probably the one that made the rules and brought us up but my father was sort of always there as well but used to be more the paper man – you know, reading the papers. I had three brothers and my role with the boys was to pick up their socks and make their beds and help my mother and help with the supper, and their role was to go out and help my father on the farm and things like that. It's funny when you look back, how much I'd actually have enjoyed going more on the farm but I just accepted it at the time.

Davina Carey-Evans, born 1965

Feet First!

I was the eldest of eight. I slept with my three sisters and what I remember best is seeing all those feet!

Priscilla Perkins, born 1920

35

CHAPTER 3
Growing up

Pembroke Dock carnival, 1955.

All-seeing Eyes

There was lots going on in Pembroke Dock in the late 1940s. The RAF and the Navy and the Army were all there. There were dances and socials and clubs and it was wonderful to be a teenager at that time, as long as you had done your homework. That's where your extended family became a burden because you couldn't do anything without somebody seeing you and your mother knowing before you got home. The limits were stated. You were given a time to come home and you were home at that time. I never minded, even years later. If I went off to Tenby for a dance my father would come to meet the bus. If anybody was with me he'd say, 'All right' and he would walk home ahead of us. It was just what you were brought up to expect. You had levels and you lived with those. There was never a reason to rebel because my parents were both reasonable. You went out with a group and you came back with the group. Sometimes my aunties would say, 'Better not bring any trouble home here,' and what did that mean? It could have been anything, couldn't it?

They had what they called a workhouse in Pembroke Dock and at one time all the people who got pregnant and had no support were plonked in there. That had been the system up to the early 1920s. It was very cruel and I don't know what happened to the babies, whether they were adopted. Women always bore the brunt of everything. It's a very true saying, a man can put his hat on and his roof is thatched, but women even today bear the responsibility.

Olwen Burton, born 1933

Student nurse Olwen 'Tommy' Thomas – later Olwen Burton – in 1950.

KO'd by a Kiss!

I had my eye on this guy in the sixth form common room and finally I got to snog him and I immediately fainted! This was my future husband. We went to this disco on a Thursday night. I chatted him up and he chatted me up and then that happened. It was the height of embarrassment. I couldn't believe it. I hadn't had much to drink, just a couple of halves of cider or whatever we had in those days. My brother hurried me off and I remember walking home being horrified thinking, how am I going to go back to school? I had to go to school next morning and face everybody. The first Friday lesson

A proud day for Herbert and Helun David when their daughter Louise (front, right) celebrated her twenty-first birthday. Louise's sisters Caroline (standing, left) and Sally joined in the fun.

was double statistics with a nice maths teacher, a roly-poly man. He handed out the homework and the first question was: State whether the following are discrete or random variables – (a) The number of girls who faint in discos! This was 9 o'clock, mind, so the story has been round the common room and this teacher had had time to go and amend his homework sheet to take account for the fact I had fainted! I just looked at him and was horrified again, and I'm horrified with it now at the age of twenty-eight.

Elizabeth Smith, born 1971

Holding Hands

Cowbridge became quite chi-chi and up-market in the '70s and a beauty and hair salon opened. When I was sixteen I got my eyebrows plucked – I thought I was so grown-up! But I definitely didn't dye my hair until I went to university, when I came up with bright orange hair. I had my first snog when I was in Standard Four in the Juniors – nothing serious! You just went behind the cattle market and held hands. I had my first real boyfriend in High School – I was in the fifth form and he was in the sixth form. He had an MGA car which he'd renovated and I felt ever so grown up. When I reached the sixth form people were having their eighteenth birthdays so there were lots of parties in houses when mums and dads were out. I used to drink dry Martini – it was great.

Louise Prynne, born 1958

Bright Yellow Hair

We have sex education at school. We had a doctor in about six months ago, talking about contraception and things like that. She handed out leaflets that made a lot of sense. My parents have never said anything, they probably know they teach us at school. I'm not really bothered about going out with someone, I've got better things to do. If I did ask a girl for a date I'd probably take her to a cinema in Builth. That would be about £3 or £4 there and back in a taxi … about £8. I once dyed my hair blond in the summer holidays. It turned out much brighter than I thought it would be – for the first couple of days it was yellow. My parents were on holiday and I was staying at my Nan's. She didn't say anything and when my parents found out they just laughed.

James Price, born 1984

Edith Knew

I was told nothing about sex. If anybody told me anything it was Edith the maid. She was brought up on a farm, one of thirteen children. She was certainly like a second mother. We didn't sleep around and of course we didn't sleep with a boy. It's quite exciting when you don't sleep with someone and I think that's

missing today. This big build-up of petting and holding hands and all those things which were good fun whereas now when I talk to young people, goodness me, in no time at all they're in bed together and I think what a shame they've missed out on that really exciting part of discovering it all. I think when the pill came in it made a big difference. It gave women the freedom to do what they wanted and I think that's not a bad thing because before, men had more freedom than women. But courtesy and all that is really lovely and the building up to sex is nice … I tried not to imagine my parents doing it and I think all children are like that.

Mair McGeever, born 1940

Courting has always been a swinging business – Mair McGeever's parents, Emyr Jones and Phyllis Pritchard, as teenagers.

We Were All At It

We were all sexually abusing each other. There were five boys older than me who would have been hauled up before a social worker now because of what they were doing when we were between the ages of five and twelve. There was an enormous amount of sex play among children. The children were in gangs and they were kicked out of the house all day by their parents and they learned about sex the normal way, through experimentation. Also we were very close to the country and life on the farms. I had friends who assisted their parents with lambing so they knew what was what, and everyone did. When my mother came to give me the obligatory 20-second reference to sex it was, 'You know boys have got these things and you know they like to do things to girls, well you mustn't let them.' I thoroughly understand President Clinton's statement that he didn't have sex with Monica Lewinsky. He had everything else except sexual intercourse. Well, that's how it was in Caernarfon throughout my teenage years, only people couldn't get their hands on cigars and when they did they smoked them!

Nerys Patterson, born 1943

Search Party

You could go anywhere without any fear at all. One Easter Sunday when I was about thirteen we walked all the way from Cardiff to Barry Island – about 10 miles from our house. We just carried on walking. We were starving when we got there. We bumped into somebody from the street where I lived and he said, 'You'd better get home or your parents are going to kill you.' We got to the top of Leckwith Hill and they were all out with their dogs looking for us. It was about seven o'clock in the evening.

Carnival day in Gabalfa, Cardiff, in the 1950s.

There was my father and a couple of my brothers and a couple of policemen, they were all over the place. They were so angry with us and so pleased to see us, we got taken home and put to bed. There used to be masses and masses of open fields and woods and we stayed out all day with a bottle of sherbet water and some bread and jam sandwiches. You'd be out about ten in the morning and you wouldn't go back until five in the evening. We'd be filthy dirty sometimes, our clothes would be torn, but we had such fun. We'd be in the fresh air enjoying ourselves and sometimes we'd be up to a bit of mischief, chasing the cows in the field or something like that, not bad things. When I was ten or eleven Cardiff was surrounded by farming but what used to be fields is all covered with houses now.

Anne Roberts, born 1939

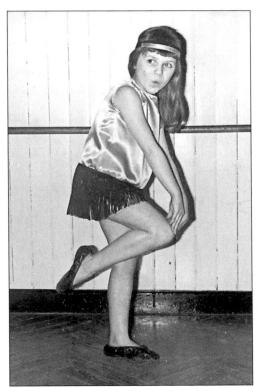

Anne Roberts' daughter Kimberley, aged nine, in 1968.

Bringing in the Coal

I grew up with a coal fire and the best coal in the world – Gwendraeth Valley anthracite coal. My father as a miner would have 13 tons of coal a year and he paid 10/- (50p) a ton during the '50s and early '60s. That's a perk the coal miners have and indeed they deserve that and more. The coal would come in big boulders. It would arrive down the end of the road because 50 yards from the house there's a huge quarry and a very narrow bridge – no vehicle could come up to the house. He used to break up the coal and wheel it up in a wheelbarrow. The garden was his pride and joy. We ate everything that he grew and likewise with the ferreting and the shooting. We ate the rabbits, the hares and the pigeons. My mother was a lovely cook and she skinned the rabbits. There was always meat and vegetables on the table and cawl [a broth] – very nutritious on a cold winter's day.

Ray Gravell, born 1952

Angel of Death

We went straight from being a child at fourteen to being an adult at fifteen. We did have our bullies, mind. I remember having problems with one person and telling my grandfather and he said 'Well, you've got to go back and fight him', as simple as that. The police sergeant lived a few doors away and he was the angel of death. You couldn't get away with it and if you smashed a window he knew you'd done something wrong and you'd get a clout across the head.

Graham Willis, born 1935

Happy to be Black

There's a picture of me when I was twelve or thirteen and I've got American tan tights, little high heels, pink lipstick and blue eye shadow and it's dreadful. My sister had gone to study art at Stoke-on-Trent and she came

The five Williams sisters with their parents, c. 1963. Back row (from left): Janice, Evelyn, Denis Williams (father), Isobel, Catherine Williams (mother). Front: Charlotte and Beatrice.

back with some Dorothy Perkins underwear with purple flowers – we'd only worn white or maybe pale pink before – and she'd bought some make-up that was the right colour for us. We'd never had the right colour before. I've always thought of those emblems of grown-upness as marking a transition in our lives. That part of our lives was quite difficult because we had nobody looking like us – five black girls growing up in Llandudno – we couldn't find products locally to do our hair and we couldn't find the right colour make-up. We were very much wanting to be the same as everybody else but not able to do that very well. At the same time I was very happy we were black because we had something really special but the two don't go together really. In terms of mixing with the boys at school, there was a kind of stand-off. You were not the kind that boys would go out with, or you weren't in that category of people. You didn't go to dances with that kind of expectation, but there were another tier of people who had left school who perhaps didn't see you in the same way, who weren't concerned about peer pressure. Jimi Hendrix was changing our world, it was becoming cool to be black. Slowly it was trickling through even to Llandudno so after my 'O' levels I started to go out with friends to coffee bars – you had them for young people in those days, which I think was very good because you didn't have to drink alcohol. I think my mother started to relax a bit more at that time.

Charlotte Williams, born 1954

Mrs Catherine Williams with daughter Charlotte in Craig-y-Don, Llandudno.

One Spoonful Too Many

My father was a very strict man and he laid rules and regulations down. When I was twenty-one I had to be in by 11 o'clock at night, not two minutes past, no excuses, and he would ground you at twenty-one. It all goes back to the war, I think, when people didn't have anything. I remember one of my brothers, when he got married he came one Sunday to tea and he took two spoonfuls of sugar and my father went beserk. They had a big argument and my father kicked him out of the house and told him don't come back any more, he was that strict. He was that type of man, a trawlerman, a hard-drinking man and he was the law in the house. There were things like ... he would have the breast of chicken and so would my mother, and the older boys had a leg and the next oldest had the wing and so on. It was the same when he came home from sea, he used to bring a lot of fish home and crabs. My father would have the heart of the crab, my older brothers the claws and the younger ones like me would have the little thin legs. I used to go shopping with my mother and we took it in turns to wash the dishes or wipe them, and my sister helped with the cooking. At the time, to be honest, I thought he was far too strict but now I realise it was the best thing he ever done, because if you don't put rules and regulations into your children when they're young you've got no chance of doing it when they're in their teens. He was a hard man, I remember having a belting many times. He had a leather belt with a metal buckle and if it came off you knew you were for it, he'd have you across the legs.

Terry Stewart, born 1943

A convivial day for customers of the Commercial Hotel, Cowbridge, as they set off for a day out in Worcester.

Shy About Sex

I think sex was the hardest thing about growing up. I couldn't talk about it with my father because it was the one thing he was shy about. They would tease you about it – I used to bath in the house and when I got to puberty it was dreadful because I had to bath in front of all my aunties. When you're thirteen and they make comments like 'Oh, you're well blessed' – well … They might think it's a great joke but to you it's an utter disaster. It was sex through a half-hinting jovial manner rather than 'let's talk about the birds and the bees.'

I started work in Aberaman Colliery at fifteen and until then I'd never seen my father naked. One day in the baths we walked into each other, both naked, and I've no doubt my father blushed much more than me. I remember his words to this day. He said, 'Oh, here you are, are you?' and he just turned around on his heel and went in a totally different direction.

Tyrone O'Sullivan, born 1946

You Built up a Picture

Nobody ever explained to me about sex. Kids talking to each other, reading things in the paper, jokes, going to the pictures under-age … you just gradually build up a picture.

Taz Lazarou, born 1955

No Birds, No Bees

Mam never talked about the birds and the bees or anything. You picked it up from school and when you were about fifteen you tried to get into the 'X' pictures. I think it's just natural. You just grow up – it's like animals, isn't it? You can't talk sex to a cow, can you, but they still give birth. My ten-year-old daughter now is having some sort of sex education at school – not the full-blown what-have-you, just introducing it slightly. Both my two girls should know. You see so many kids at sixteen, fifteen, even thirteen having babies, which I think is disgusting really.

Michael Crane, born 1966

Separate Sessions

I remember these lessons, the term before I went to secondary school. The girls went into the hall and the boys went in separately, and we were intrigued to know what the boys were being told. We had a very open family and I knew that periods were going to happen and how babies were made – not the relationship stuff, just the mechanics of it – so I was amazed to find some of the girls knew nothing at all. The teacher said, 'Does any girl not know about periods?' and the girls put up their hands!

Dr Amanda Kirby, born 1959

I Was Horrified

My mother taught me about periods when I was about ten. She said blood comes from you but for a long time I thought it came from your navel. I never realised where it could come from. In science and biology the teacher

Menai Bridge Carnival in 1999 – its fiftieth year – with Danielle Crane, Queen of the Menai Straits, and her court.

Two-year-old Kerry Crane in the Tinkerbell costume that won her the fancy dress competition at Menai Bridge Carnival, 1999.

gave us a book all about frogs and what they did, then it moved to cows and the next one was human beings and we had to take this book home to read. I must have been about twelve or thirteen and I was absolutely horrified and threw the book across the room thinking, 'I'm never going to do that!' We never discussed it in biology afterwards.

Jean Williams, born 1950.

CHAPTER 4

Living together

Herbert David and Helun Greenwood on their wedding day in Cowbridge, June 1954.

My Husband Was a Hero

I was thirty-six when I conceived – a late starter! We've got twin daughters. My husband decided he was quite happy to have a career break so at eleven weeks I went back to work and he stayed home and looked after them. Of course, because he's a bloke everyone took pity on him and rallied round. All the blokes thought he was an absolute hero. I think it was quite isolating for him because as a woman you'll go to toddler groups and coffee mornings but Andrew wasn't keen to get into that, but he was quite happy. What we find very strange is that although he was home with the girls for three years, if they have an upset or a fall they say,

Gwen Hughes's grandparents, Capt. William Pritchard and his wife, aboard ship.

'We want Mum.' It must be genetic.

Louise Prynne, born 1958

Burning the Bacon

Nain (Grandmother) Pritchard and Taid fell out. I was told it was because she burnt his bacon one morning and lost her temper and went to live with her widowed sister and her bachelor brother. She stayed away for seven years. She would walk all the way round the village to get to the shops rather than walk past the house where Taid lived. Nain Pritchard was a very strong personality. Auntie Maggie used to say, 'If she could go to heaven with a bottle of wine she'd want to come away', meaning she was never contented.

Gwen Hughes, born 1933

It's Worked Out Fine

I was 36 when I got married. No, I was not romantic. I was working in Coed Ely Colliery and had this person next to me who kept on and on about his daughter so one day I said to him, 'I'll come up and take her off your hands, Johnny,' joking like. Well, I'd been to sea and had my own boat in Swansea, going fishing every weekend. I used to go round the valleys on a Sunday night, flogging fish, and I happened to meet Johnny in Treherbert one day. 'Come and meet the daughter' he said, so I met the daughter and now we're married with three kids. We've been married twenty-one years, never no problems. It

A domestic scene from 1958; Mrs Gwen Hughes is busy in her kitchen.

worked out rather nice, that did.

Dai Lawrence, born 1942

When Two People Click

I had my first daughter before I was married. I was engaged to the chap, he was a little bit older than me. I got very tempted the one night and gave in, and I was just unfortunate enough to get pregnant. It caused a big scandal in the family as in them days it just wasn't done. But I didn't want to marry him just because I was pregnant. I put myself in Northlands, it was a private nursing home with a part at the back for unmarried mothers to have their babies and put them up for adoption. I mean, there was a lot of it going on then even though it was a scandal. I was going to have my child adopted but when it actually came I couldn't do it, so one of

Anne Beam was twenty-one when she married Ron Roberts at Cardiff Register Office in 1960 to become Mrs Anne Roberts.

my sisters said 'You can come and live with us if you want to, and as soon as the baby's old enough you can go to work and I'll look after the baby in the daytime,' and that's what we did. They kept a pub and that's where I met my first husband, Ron. I used to do a few evenings behind the bar to earn some extra money. He was divorced – I've mostly gone for an older man, until now I suppose. When I was young I was looking for a father figure. Ron was a long distance lorry driver who used to come into the pub and chat to me … It was after my twenty-first birthday when he said, 'Would you like to come for a drink with me?' and the first night we went out together he asked me to marry him and I accepted. We got married and were very happy together. I'd always liked him and he was so easy to talk to and I felt so much at ease with him and so comfortable and when he touched me my whole body tingled, you know what I mean? There's so many different kinds of love. You can work at it and grow into it but I think the best love of all is the love when two people just sort of click. It's like putting two pieces of a jigsaw together.

Anne Roberts, born 1939

Old Tradition

I'm old-fashioned. I believe in three things – legal marriage not partners, being churched when you have a child, and proper funerals. But everything's changed over the years. Now, some years ago my brother's wife had a baby, Charlene, and she said to the vicar, 'I'd like to be churched' and he said 'What's that?' She told him, 'We've always had it,

whenever us show women have a baby we don't believe in putting outside until we've been churched.' He had to look it up. It's a tradition that a woman would go to church and thank God for the deliverance of the baby and herself.

Rebecca (Becky) Scarrott, born 1925

It's Just Too Easy

A month after we bought a house my husband told me he didn't feel about marriage the way he thought he would feel. His exact words were, 'I can either live the life I've been given or make the best of things.' I think nowadays it's too easy. People expect too much. The break-up of the marriage was obviously half my fault but I think it's a shame we never went to counsellors, or whatever you do. One day to my mind everything was perfect and the next day he was gone. My first reaction was, hang on a sec', come back, but there's literally nothing you can do.

Davina Carey-Evans, born 1965

I Died Inside

When we got married thirty-one years ago we had nothing, and nobody else had either. We started with a three-piece suite, a standard lamp and a mattress. Everything we acquired became precious to us and there was something to look forward to. I didn't allow our two daughters to have television in their bedrooms when they were doing their 'A' levels because you can't work and watch, but now I think perhaps I was wrong because I found all their friends had one. I just worry, I still do. One of my daughters is living in New Zealand. I found that very difficult. I said, 'Go and have a lovely time' and died inside for six months.

Sally Pryce, born 1945

Why Bother to Marry?

When I was nineteen my girlfriend was sixteen and I moved out from the council house where I'd been living with my parents to a flat. I had a job and I just spent more and more time with my girl in Menai Bridge and when I was about twenty-one I moved in with her in her mother's house. Her mother took to me as if I was one of her own because I was working and she could see her daughter was happy and I did things about the house because her husband was quite ill. It was a sign of the times – everything was changing in those days. When my brother was courting – he's six years older than me – he was hardly ever let into the house and the girl's mother didn't really accept him until they were married. That was eighteen years ago but everything seemed to change – you'd see people living together and not being married. There's me, you see – I'm not married. I've been with her thirteen years and we've got two daughters. These days people think of it just as something on a piece of paper to say you're married. You've got just as much rights now living together as you have if you're married. There's no difference really.

Michael Crane, born 1966

Michael Crane and his partner Julie.

Alien to My Nature

I'm a traditionalist. I believe in the sanctity of marriage, and that's the way that families should be brought up. Gays and lesbians are totally alien to my nature. I can't condone it [homosexual behaviour]. I think it's morally wrong. I have a sadness that they are made differently but please don't foist it on the rest of us because we don't want it.

John Williams, born 1939

Putting Up With Each Other

The best thing about marriage is to have someone with you all the way. I think it's just great to have a mate because you have to face up to loads of difficult things. You set up home and have children and it's not easy and a lot of people think it's just a lot of give and take. You get to know your own weaknesses and wonder how the hell he can put up with you, but then you think … well, you've got to put up with him.

Mair McGeever, born 1940

She'd Have Killed Me!

I think my mother would have killed me if I'd gone to live with my wife before we got married – that's a Welsh chapel upbringing for you! Saying that,

A day out at Porthcawl for Graham Harris's great-grandparents – John Evan Jones and his wife Mary Hannah, of Resolven.

mind, perhaps it's a good idea for some people to live together and find out what their partner is like – but then again, maybe that's too easy because if you're married, you've got to work at it. We've had our disagreements but I've never gone to sleep not talking to my wife. We've had a couple of arguments but anything severe, she just don't talk to me, that's all! I had a very stable upbringing, no problems at all. What makes a partnership work? I think you've got to work hard at it, that's very important. In fact when I got married – this is sheer horror – I sat down and asked her to cut my toe nails because that was always one of the things my mother used to do. Pampered, that's what I was. One thing I do is make cups of tea, because my wife detests making them.

Graham Harris, born 1960

Starry-Eyed Bride

Divorce has been made too easy, perhaps. If you give up at the first hurdle in marriage and say 'Blow it, I think I'll find somebody else' or 'I'd like to be on my own', perhaps a good marriage will go down the drain just for the want of making an effort. Putting up with the foibles and funny ways about a person – you can't like everything about them – is all part of marriage. My husband doesn't like everything about me, I suppose, but we've been married fifty-one years. There've been hard years and easy years but I think marriage is a good thing and I think it should stay. I think children are the ones that come out worse in a divorce. They lose their

Daddy or their Mummy and they can't understand why and they think it's their fault. I think people should really work at a marriage. It's a gamble for everyone. You've got this starry-eyed concept of marriage, that everything will be hunky-dory, all love and kisses, but it's been hard – not because my husband wasn't the right man for me but because I went into marriage expecting it to be all bliss but it wasn't and it isn't even today but it's been worthwhile.

Alethea Jones, born 1928

I Fell For Her

I met my wife in 1964 in a pub in Swansea called the Park Hotel – it's a bank now. They had pop groups upstairs and there was a gentlemen's toilet in the corner. My wife was sitting down and as I walked past she stuck a leg out and tripped me up. That's what I always say – I fell for her!

Terry Stewart, born 1943

Practical Proposal

My parents adored one another although my father was seventeen years older than my mother . They had a very positive symbiosis, if that's the right word, for those days. When my father decided to do things he did them, so when he decided to get married and that she was the girl he wanted, he got himself asked to her house by her

Mrs Winifred Evans of Resolven with her three sons and six daughters.

Charles Thomas, Lord Mayor of Swansea, and Mrs Doreen Thomas, Lady Mayoress, 1983.

parents – that's how things were then – and apparently his courtship consisted mainly of saying, 'Well, Judy, you know what I've come here for.' He was very awkward like that, none of this bending on your knee thing – just practical!

Lord Raglan, born 1927

Snakes Alive!

I think the chances of me having a wife are very slim indeed because the job I hope to have when I'm older is studying reptiles and not many women would find that very appealing.

Oliver Price, born 1985

Career Woman

I want a husband and I want to be a career woman – I want both, and I want three kids. I don't want to have a nanny looking after my children and I do think that the way they had was right in the olden days. I'm not saying it's always the mother who should look after the children but one of the parents should, instead of getting an outsider. I think it's good now that a lot of men are doing things that women used to do.

Lizzie Greenaway, born 1985

Am I Invisible?

Life has changed completely. The old people stick together but there's a gulf between the young and the old because of their differing life styles. I love people – I love young people and children – but the young don't like the old for some reason. I go up to the school sometimes to fetch my little granddaughter. The young mothers are there but they don't want to talk to me or anyone else my age. Sometimes I walk along the road and say 'Good morning' – not a sound, not a smile and I think to myself, 'Well, don't then.' I've gone now that I feel like that, you know – I go up to a friend and say, 'Can you see me? Am I here? I think I'm invisible because I'm saying hello to people and they don't answer me back.'

Alethea Jones, born 1928

Cracking Round the Seams

My parents are still happily married after nearly fifty years together but like any other marriage it's had its ups and downs. I can remember them arguing and my mother once threw a pot across the room and it had these little pebbles in it rather than soil and they were scattered everywhere. But on the whole it's been a very good, sound marriage. You look back and see your own marriage reflected in theirs and you realise they didn't argue much at all really. Divorce was very uncommon when I was at school, but in my daughter's class probably a third of the girls have parents who are divorced or separated. This often comes after fifteen or twenty years, when the marriage is cracking a little around the seams.

Dr Amanda Kirby, born 1959

Dennis Williams and Catherine Alice Hughes on their wedding day in 1947.

55

CHAPTER 5

Belonging

Sisters Janice, Evelyn, Beatrice and Charlotte Williams with their mother Mrs Catherine Williams (front row, left) and her sisters Ethel and Enid.

Welsh, Not British

I'm Welsh, 110%. I don't think I've ever felt British. I've been an internationalist all my life, I feel a part of the world, but I definitely feel more comfortable being a European than British. I wouldn't want to be part of a nation that hasn't played what I'd call a sympathetic role in the world. I know other countries have got a similar sort of history but I would say I'd rather be a European than British. If someone called himself British I think that predominantly he'd be English.

My great-grandfather on my father's side came from Ireland – a little place near Cork. He came over in the 1850s, landed in Pembroke Dock and went for a job in Cardiff Castle, working on the land and and grounds. Eventually Lord Aberdare employed him so that's how he found himself up in the Welsh valleys. He married my great-grandmother and that's the Irish part of me, and I like that. I'm 110% Welsh so the Irish part has to be added on. You'd have to make me a person of 120% or 130%.

Tyrone O'Sullivan, born 1946

Nobody Else Looked Like Us

My Mum's from Bethesda – she's Welsh-speaking – and my father's from the Caribbean. He was on a British scholarship studying art in London and they met there. My father's an archaeologist and my earliest memories are of him working in Africa. We'd been travelling around as little children and my mother decided we should have a home somewhere to attach us to a community, so she bought a house in Llandudno. My Mum is Welsh not only in terms of her language but of her whole cultural heritage. Llandudno itself isn't particularly Welsh in those terms. It isn't an area where there are a lot of Welsh speakers so she was a little bit of an oddity. She was a minority herself if you define Welshness in that way. We had the sense that the real Welsh people were the Welsh speakers like her, though I later came to revise that. I saw myself as black before I saw myself as Welsh. I'd say I was very ambivalent about this. There were lots of things that were comfortable and happy about seeing yourself as black in our house, but at school and so on it was something you carried with you as a bit of a burden. We were the only black family, we were the only people we saw who looked like us. There was no role model, nobody really then on television, nobody to identify with. It was a totally isolated upbringing.

In terms of my sense of being a Welsh person … this is a claim that I've made very strongly as an adult rather than as a child. In our minds there was no such thing as black Welsh. I know now that there's black Welsh in Cardiff but I didn't know it then. As an adult I've tried hard to shift people's perception of me as an outsider. I make my claim to be Welsh in all sorts of ways but it's still a challenge.

Charlotte Williams, born 1954

A street party in Craddock Street, Riverside, Cardiff, for the wedding of Prince Charles and Lady Diana.

Every Word Was in English

We were taught in English, every word in English even in the elementary school. English people living here now don't realise what we had to do. They complain about their children having to take Welsh lessons, well they don't have to do half as much as we had to speak English. We spoke Welsh at home, we went to Sunday school and chapel, everything was Welsh, we played in Welsh. Then as soon as we went into the classroom we were in English and Welsh teachers spoke English to us.

Hannah Rowlands, born 1909

Only the Servants Spoke Welsh

My mother is an Anglesey girl and her first language is Welsh. My father is 100% Welsh as well but he was brought up in London and – this is how it's been explained to me – Welsh in London was the language that the servants spoke. His parents always spoke Welsh together but they enjoyed having it because the English people didn't understand them. They didn't see the necessity for their four children to have the language, yet they used to come back here [to Cricieth] every summer for their holidays. A lot of the people my father played with in the summer are still here and they don't speak Welsh, even though they have lived here all their lives. It's funny, there was a generation that considered it ... well ... I suppose it was a snobbery thing here. There's no polite way of putting it. It was considered a working-class language and it's wonderful to see how it's changed. In some ways it's quite surprising coming back to Wales now because in Spain it's all pro-Europe. Spanish schoolchildren have two hours of English every afternoon from the age of three and when they're seven they start having French so they'll be very much European children. Now my children are back in Cricieth they're being taught in Welsh, OK? It's great, it's wonderful, but you can't help wondering what if your child wants to go and work in Cardiff or London or Manchester or Liverpool when you have nothing but one language ... and English especially is very much the business language and it's a difficult language

Farmer William Edwards with his gun dog Scramble.

Llanberis Show, 1937.

to read. Probably all Welsh people of my generation will tell you that they are out there in their jobs, out of Wales and their written English is so behind, or not so good as it should be. I remember going to London for my first job, I was eighteen, and the man I worked with couldn't believe I got my p's and b's wrong every single time. I was very lucky because he sat with me for a whole year getting me to do it the right way round.

Davina Carey-Evans, born 1965

Welsh Italians

My parents came to live in Wales from Italy just before the First World War. My father was only twelve. His elder brother was already here. Most of the Italians who came to Britain at that time actually walked through Switzerland and France. They were quite proud – they wouldn't want anything for nothing. They would offer to clean out the stables or chop some wood in exchange for a meal and as long as they could sleep in a barn that's all they wanted. After crossing the Channel most of them headed for London. Some of them thought they'd got to America because they'd been conned by the shipping people. Some stayed in London but a lot of them couldn't connect with the English mentality so they kept on walking. They ended up in Scotland or came down to Wales and they found that the Celtic mind was more in tune

The Supper Bar in Gwendoline Street, Trenewydd, Rhondda, c. 1930.

The Cosy Café in Bute Street, Treherbert, Rhondda, c. 1951. Proprietor Vittorio (Vic) Basini is on the extreme right, next to Mrs Santina Basini. Romeo Basini is on the extreme left.

with the Latin attitude. It could be something to do also with the fact that London was a prosperous city and in the Rhondda the people were hard-working and quite poor, like the Italians, so there was a link – maybe emotional is the wrong word – but a definite link in their outlook that they had to work hard in order to get somewhere. They rented front rooms to open cafés and worked all hours. They were open when the miners set off for the first shift at 4 o'clock in the morning, and when they came home they were still open. They had no social life, partly because of the language. They preferred to marry Italian girls, so they had this tribal thing. Any money they made they reinvested in the business. Instead of the original rough wooden tables they had marble tables. The primitive chairs became benches. One of the first things I remember selling was a packet of twist [tobacco] to a miner for 1/- [5p]. They used to chew it in the mines so that they could spit the dust out in their saliva. That way it didn't get to their lungs. There were 52 mines in the Rhondda and 54 cafés. Now the mines have gone and you've probably got 15 cafés.

Romeo Basini, born 1937

A Plague On Both Your Houses

My family were from these parts. They had been wandering around Gloucestershire and south-east Wales for about 700 years, I suppose. One of my ancestors married the heiress of Raglan Castle about 1450 and that's how my immediate family came into these parts. They lived at the castle until Cromwell knocked it down.

I feel neither Welsh nor English, I must say … a plague upon both of them. I wish the Welsh Assembly hadn't come about but I think it was inevitable in the long run from the time that a Minister for Welsh Affairs was appointed in 1952. Once the geographical area of Wales was designated as a separate administrative entity there was no point at which you could say they should not be responsible for this or responsible for that. You'll hear a lot from nationalists now that it's an insult to Wales that we haven't got these or those powers and in a sense they're quite right – I don't know about insult but I think that nobody will be able to draw a line either with Scotland or Wales as to how far the powers of these parliaments will go.

Lord Raglan, born 1927

All Europeans Now

I would say without hesitation that I'm Welsh although I was born in England. It isn't the place of birth that matters, it's the influence that counts. I was brought up in a Welsh home and went to a Welsh Sunday school and was immersed in the Welsh Labour tradition. When I went to Ruskin College I was more a Welshman than ever. Now I do feel European and I'll tell you why. After I'd been in the European Parliament for a while, mixing freely with

Candyfloss delight for Mair Jones and her sister Nan, with their Uncle Ted.

Italians, Spanish, Portuguese and Uncle Tom Cobley and all I thought, there's no difference between us. We've got the same basic hopes of life and living. European, yes, but being European isn't belonging to a country, it's a state of mind. I'm Welsh, but the great thing about being Welsh is that I'm able to make my contribution to European society without let or hindrance.

David Morris, born 1931

Between Two Cultures

I class myself as a Welsh Greek. I'm very much a part of the Welsh community when I'm outside that front door and everything that happens in Wales is important to me because if things are ticking here my family's going to tick too. Inside I go back to my roots – I'm Greek from Cyprus. My children were all born here but I think it's important to teach them where I came from – my culture, my roots.

Taz Lazarou, born 1955

Never Stood for 'The Queen'

I'm 100% pure Welsh as far as I know. I was born in 1940 and we didn't love the English very much. It would be very difficult to stand up for *God Save the Queen*. I'll do it today though I don't enjoy it, but in those days one would never have done it. Mind, when you marry an Englishman and he's one-quarter Irish it helps!

Mair McGeever, born 1940

63

Fred Lawes – Alfred Lawes' father - who was a miner in Maerdy, Rhondda.

Just Picked Up Welsh

Dad's from Liverpool and Mum's from a little village called Llanberis, just outside Caernarfon. I think me Dad was on National Service down in Betws-y-coed. Mum worked in a café in Caernarfon when they met. Dad used to be a long-distance bus driver but he finished there and went on the local routes. He took to Welsh as if it was natural. He speaks fluent Welsh – unbelievable. He just picked it up. Mam speaks Welsh of course and her Mam couldn't speak a word of English. I remember Nan when I was about four – it was Welsh, Welsh, Welsh. Not that she was against the English – she was just Welsh through and through. I was brought up Welsh and English. My two brothers can't speak Welsh at all, but me and my sister can. We used to speak with Mam in Welsh and they wouldn't have a clue. There's six years between us and in that time they put more Welsh into the school. Everything was English in our estate when they were younger. I wouldn't say I was British, I'd just say Welsh. Like when we go abroad and people say 'Where are you from?' I say Wales and they say, 'Do you mean England?' and I say no. It's as if people abroad think England's Great Britain. That's what used to get to me see, but it's getting better.

Michael Crane, born 1966

My Colour's No Problem

I would say mostly I'm a boy from Maerdy in the Rhondda, that's who I am. The fact is my father was a West Indian and my mother came from Cardiff. That doesn't matter at all here in the Rhondda because I'm Alfie Lawes of Maerdy, that's how they know me. My colour doesn't matter one iota. I'm a governor of two schools and chairman of the local community association and I hold high office in the Royal Ancient Order of Buffalos. If they didn't like me they wouldn't ask me to do all those things, would they? Back in 1912 my father was working on the ships coming into Cardiff, that was their home port. He was a member of the seafarers' union, but they brought in coolie labour, cheap labour to take coal from Cardiff so naturally they all had the sack. My father and his friends said, 'We've been carrying coal all round the world and it comes from down there somewhere,' so they caught trains and eventually got to Maerdy. They were still sitting in the carriage when the stationmaster comes in and says, 'Hullo, boys, what are you doing here? You're a long way from home.' 'Oh, we've come to work – to cut the coal we've been carrying all round the world,' they tell him. 'We've all had the sack because we're in the union.' 'Best thing for you is see the people at Maerdy Hall,' says the stationmaster. 'They're sure to fix you up.' Well, these were the first black faces they'd ever seen in the Valleys but when they heard about them being union members they said, 'You've come to the right place' and believe it or not all five of them were taken on. No questions asked. They were taken in as lodgers by local people. It was really something to my

Mrs Louise Lawes with her daughter Florence and son Dominic in 1930.

Alfred Lawes with his daughter, Mrs Ann Phillips.

father, being accepted as part of the family, but when it came to such things as bathing in front of the fire … the men would all do that and the neighbours would be in and out talking, and whoever came in just grabbed the flannel to wash their back … it took a little while for them to get used to that. But they were taken into Maerdy just as people and they were judged not on their colour but the fact they were men and willing to work down the pit.

I was born in a cellar in Royal Cottages. My father was Daddy Lawes and my mother was Bopa Lawes – that's how they were known. As you know, in Wales there's always a Bopa. If someone's ill or dying, 'Call Bopa Lawes.' My father used to tell stories about the sea – many a time I'd see him there, sitting outside the door telling the children stories – some of them were fantasised but they really loved them! All I know about my father's homeland is that it was St Kitts in the West Indies. He never went back. This is my home and everybody knows it.

Alfred Lawes, born 1919

CHAPTER 6
Work

Shearing on Mynydd Hiraethog, Denbighshire, before 1921.

Robert Hughes, facing the camera on a busy day of sheep shearing at Cwm, Capel Curig, *c.* 1925.

Ploughing and Planting

I remember the threshing machines going around – steam engines, you know. Dai Bach yr Engine used to own them – he came from Llanegryn. The machine had a big steam boiler and a big fly wheel and it was drawn by horses, you see – they needed about six horses to shift it. Now they have these combine harvesters – there's no threshing goes on really. My sisters did milking and things like that. I was ploughing and planting potatoes, swedes – plenty to do, carting manure. I had a single furrow plough with two heavy horses. There used to be ploughing matches in the old days but I didn't bother with that, you know. You had to get a special plough for that – what we used to call the Scotch plough.

Dewi Evans, born 1915

Human Ballast

I worked in Cardiff docks from 1925 till 1988. I was a crane driver, working cargoes of iron ore. My father was a storeman on the same wharf for fifty-six years. Grandad, who was born in the year of the potato blight in Ireland, wanted to emigrate to New York but the ship he was on foundered in the Irish Sea and they landed in Milford Haven. They called them human ballast in those days. Some people had an ingenious idea – instead of putting, say, manganese ore for bottom storage they put Irish immigrants desperate to get away from the potato blight. They put them down the holds of the ships as ballast and let them travel free. All they had between them and the steel plates in the bottom of the ship was a bit of pathetic rag or an old coat. For years when I was an apprentice, my mother

68

used to give me a 2lb loaf of wholemeal bread and half a pound of cheese and that would make sandwiches for breakfast and dinner. My appetite was so ravenous I had a job to keep any for dinner – I ate all of it for breakfast! I just kept on working – I loved the job. I was on my own. I was in the open air. And there was good money to be earned. In my sixties I had a lovely job, a lovely crane and the boss said, 'Age is nothing to you.' When I was seventy-three they sent me to work in Ebbw Vale every year. The children would look up at me on their way home from school and say, 'What's the weather like up there, guv?' Then I wrote to the Commercial Dry Dock and had a wonderful time. I was on their books for five or six years at least. I helped to convert two ocean-going trawlers for the Falklands War. And after that I told them, if you ever need me for holiday relief or anything else just let me know. I had a phone call from the dry dock asking me to go in when I was in my eighty-first year, and I went. There was a piece in the Western Mail saying I was the oldest crane driver in the world. And I'm still on their books, mind you!

William (Bill) O'Neill, born 1908

Two Cows, Seven Acres

Uncle John was a quarryman and left for work about seven, and during the haymaking time he'd be up at three or four. They had two cows and seven

Bill O'Neill, still driving his crane in Cardiff docks at the age of seventy-five in 1983.

acres and he'd cut the two or three fields with a scythe, and all the other farmers did the same. They'd take it in turns in the evenings and over weekends – not Sundays of course – to help one another with the haymaking and then everybody would eat potatoes and buttermilk and rice pudding with lots of currants in it and they'd go from farm to farm. I'd go with them. It was great fun.

Gwen Hughes, born 1933

The Pits Shut Down

When I was fifteen I went to work in the fitting shop of the local iron mine and after passing out [of my apprenticeship] I worked for the NCB in Llanharan Colliery. I worked there till it closed in 1962 and then I went with a contracting firm and worked all over the place – the tin mines in Cornwall, the north-bound Blackwall Tunnel in London – we drove that fellow through. I went back to the NCB in '74 and said, 'That's it.' I was going to work till I was sixty-five and then retire, but of course that bitch Maggie [Thatcher] come along and shut the pits down, and we ended up out of work. She ruined the country without a doubt, well she ruined Wales.

Dai Lawrence, born 1942

Dockland 'Judge'

I'm seventy-one years of age. I spent nearly all my working life in the port of Swansea. I worked as a crane driver

The washery at Tower Colliery – the last deep mine in the South Wales coalfield, saved from closure through being taken over by the men themselves.

Swansea dockers sitting on a load of pig iron, mid-1960s.

Tawe ferryman David Clarke (left) and his son – also David - took workmen across the river Tawe in Swansea.

on the docks. I was a messenger boy at the beginning of the war and progressed from there. When you think of the trade that used to be there … there were 1,400 dockers – crane drivers, talleymen, tugboatmen, coal trimmers, maintenance men. Every day was different, every ship was different. You could always look out and see the ships at anchor in the bay, and you could learn something every day of your life. You worked with all kinds of individuals – there were hard characters, there were gentle characters. You had fathers whose sons were doctors and barristers and lawyers, and a lot of the men you worked with had nicknames – The Moving Bush, Silent Night, African Dan, The Silver Tongue, Bonzo, Bampy. Those were affectionate names, and when I became a magistrate as years went on, although people knew me as Charlie Thomas they would say, 'Anyone know where The Judge is working?' The dock industry was made up of father and son. When I was in the crane my Uncle Wally would be a hatchway man, my brother Jack would be down the lower hold, my Uncle Ernie would be ashore as a talleyman and my Uncle Jim would be bringing the gear to the side for you to work. So that was the type of thing that happened every day of your life, fathers, sons, brothers, uncles – they all worked together and you had to be careful what you said to

The *Santa Rosa* – one of the first American troop ships into Swansea during the Second World War.

National Federation of Young Farmers' Clubs

WALES

WILLIAM EDWARDS

LLANGEFNI Y.F.C.

Penbol,
Rhosgoch,
Anglesey,
North Wales.

1969 Delegate to Canada

The Young Farmers' Club delegate card that William Edwards took to Canada in 1969.

A proud moment for William Edwards at Llanrwst Show, standing just behind his Charolais bull that went on to become supreme champion of Wales in 1980. Stockman William Owen is on the right.

each other or they'd tell you off.

Charles Thomas, born 1928

Feeding the Men

Most farmers' wives go out to work now – they have to, to survive. In the old days the farmer's wife would be at home making the men tea. When I married, at shearing time you'd have fifteen men to lunch, they'd be there again for tea and all through the harvest you'd be feeding the men. It changes the whole atmosphere of a farm when the men bring their own food for lunch and tea. It's not the same.

Jenny Edwards, born 1953

Work's Making Us Ill

The pace of work has almost taken us over, so you get more and more people talking about the pressures of work. Work is making us ill and it might be we'll decide to jump off collectively, not just as women but as workers. We might decide we want to work in a different way, share the work out with those who don't have access to work, or work more flexibly. I don't think we can go on working at the pace we're going now. People aren't seeing themselves as whole persons, they're seeing themselves as work machines or maybe appendages of a greater work machine.

Charlotte Williams, born 1954

Boys on Strike

I was one of those children who never sat the eleven-plus. My father and mother didn't consider education all that important. I would leave school at fourteen and go into a job and bring home money – that was the general feeling at the time, and that's what I did. I left school at fourteen and went to work in a foundry and brought home 12/6 [62p] for a 48-hour week. I was given two bob [10p] a week pocket money and the rest went to my mother. For the first month I was errand boy and then general labourer. It was very hard work. I led my first strike at fifteen because of the heat. We were working on spot welding machines and they gave off molten metal which burned your hands, burned your clothes. We said we wanted gloves and aprons but the manager, Mr Burns, wouldn't give them to us so I said, 'Come on boys, down tools.' I remember my father pleading with me, then the shop steward pleading with me but we refused to work. The foreman, who was my uncle, came along and tried to persuade us to go back to work but we didn't. Two days later we had gloves and aprons. That was the first successful strike by young people in that foundry.

David Morris, born 1931

Culture Shock

I left school at 15 and went to work in a factory making cigarette papers. I was very naïve and found myself with these two bullies so I packed in the job after four days. Then I went to a glove

Student nurses in Swansea in the 1950s. Olwen 'Tommy' Thomas – later Mrs Olwen Burton – is second from the right in the front row.

factory and they were a nice bunch and later I worked in the paper mills. It was poor pay but better conditions. Working in a factory was a real education for me. When I began I was religious and didn't swear and I was put with this girl from the Rhondda and every other word was effing this and effing that. She had her hair peroxide dyed and she was fantastic, it was like an awakening. The older girls used to say to me, 'Run over the shop and do this and do that' but after a couple of weeks this other girl would say, 'Go your effing self,' and I'd be amazed that she had that kind of courage, so I learned a lot from that. It was a real culture shock.

Jean Williams, born 1950

CHAPTER 7
Money

Fairways in Tyla Rhosyr, Cowbridge – the three-bedroom detached house which local builder Robert Thomas built for £2,800 on land which butcher Herbert David bought for £150 in 1954.

No money worries for these youngsters! Mandy Greenwood (front) and her cousin Louise spill off their toboggan in the 'big snow' of 1963 in Cowbridge.

Credit Was Out

I was one of three girls. We always had pocket money – we didn't have to do jobs to get it. Then there was birthday money and Christmas. I was deemed the best one for saving and had about £350 in the bank when I was about 10. My ambition was to have £1,000 in the bank when I was 18 and I actually made it. That was with the Saturday jobs I was doing from the age of sixteen, which paid about 30p an hour – the going rate. Credit isn't part of my father's vocabulary at all. He actually paid cash for his house – he never had a mortgage. 'If you can't afford it you don't have it' – that was his philosophy, and my Mum shared it. It's different with us – we've got into the monthly salary thing. Our household bills are paid by direct debit. You don't see the money, it just happens. If you want something you can buy it at nought per cent interest over six months. We fall into that trap. Mind, we try to manage it as sensibly as we can.

Louise Prynne, born 1958

Errand Boy

When I was at school I used to deliver groceries around the houses with a carrier bike. The bike was too big for me so I pushed it because I couldn't get my leg over the crossbar. It tipped up very often. I used to kick the fork out and stand it upright, and all the groceries would be in the basket. I also washed bottles

Daisy Evans – 'I get 90p because I'm nine'

at a chemist's to earn a bit more pocket money. A lot of my school friends would get up early to go to Swansea fish market. They'd earn a few shillings trucking fish to the vans. You'd see youngsters up at five in the morning and then going to school. It was nothing to sit next to a boy smelling of fish, bless 'em.

Charles Thomas, born 1928

I Blame the Banks

When we married we were really, really hard up and we rented a horrible place for five years. I'd buy a second-hand pram because we didn't have the money for a posh pram. I tend to think the banks are to blame for the new attitude to money. You feel awful if you're in the red but the banks just seem to encourage this. I get things through the post offering me loans and students are allowed to borrow and I don't think the banks have got a conscience.

Gwen Hughes, born 1933

Credit Card Fears

I've never been able to save for what I want. I bought the furniture on HP because it was nought per cent finance. If I'd saved it, it would have gone by the time I could afford it. I've got a credit card but it would worry me terribly if I owed a lot of money.

Sally Pryce, born 1945

Sweet Money

I get 90p pocket money 'cos I'm nine. I spend it all on sweets – strawberries and cream, I love them. I get about twenty for 90p. I've got a bank account and a post office account. I've got about £35 in my bank account. Mr Taid – he's dead now – used to come down to us when we were in Cardiff and give us money every time. He'd give us 20p. We'd have money to put into our account and money for Christmas and birthdays and stuff so I was saving quite a lot. It's worth it. I'd like to earn a lot of money when I grow up but it's not important to be rich.

Daisy Evans, born 1990

Mum Paid the Bills

We had pocket money and then I had an allowance as I grew up. My parents were careful with money and we felt my Dad, who was an anaesthetist, had to work hard but we lived very comfortably. My Mum always did the household bills – I can picture her now, sitting at the table going through them. I remember going to the butchers with them – they would choose the meat and make an order, and the butcher would send it round. It was the same with the fruit and veg. I can remember these people quite clearly – they were the owners of the shops. The fruit and veg and so on would come in boxes and it would be wrapped in greaseproof paper, and the bill would be there at the side. I don't remember

The changing scene at 1 and 3 Pool Street, Caernarfon, between the two world wars.

going to supermarkets much as a child –
that's something else that's changed!

Dr Amanda Kirby, born 1959

Nobody Spoke About Money

Nearly all the men worked in the
quarries in Bethesda and you didn't
have anybody trying to be better than
anybody else. Oh, they were hard times.
I knew my friend Phyl had money but it
was never talked about, she lived
exactly the same as the rest of us. Every
time I went to school to play hockey my
mother gave me 2/6 [12p] 'in case
something happened, but remember
you've got to bring it back.' She didn't
want me to have less than anyone else
but if something did happen I don't
know what I'd have done. I'd have been
afraid of going home without the
money!

Hannah Rowlands, born 1909

The Day Mam Panicked

I became aware of money at an early
age when my mother panicked one
day and a quarrel developed. My mother
opened the mail, tore a bill up and
threw it down the toilet pan. It was a
bill for £30 or £40 from the Co-op in
Kidwelly and my father was in a rage.
He never physically hit my mother but
verbally he was in a rage. He was telling
me my mother hadn't paid the bill and
£30 was a huge amount then.

Ray Gravell, born 1952

CHAPTER 8
Social problems

Were there fewer social problems then? Coronation Day celebrations in Morris Lane School in Swansea, 1953.

Please Come Quickly!

I had a break-in once. I was sleeping in the back bedroom and heard the glass falling on the sill and somebody coming in. I thought to myself, 'If I ring up from here they'll come and take the phone from me,' so I came from there very quickly. I dialled 999 and said 'Oh please come, they're breaking my window, there's somebody coming in, please come quickly.' They said, 'We'll be there in no time, Mrs Rowlands, don't upset yourself.' The police came and the ones who'd broken in went full speed and the police went after them. They'd taken my rings that were on the dressing table and some money I had in the drawer and that's all. 3 o'clock on a Sunday morning, that's when it was. I never got my rings back. They're gone. I was all right when it happened but I think it's had some effect on me since, you know.

Hannah Rowlands, born 1909

Absent Parents

In my twenty-five years as a magistrate I've seen youngsters come to court at times accompanied by a local authority person, not their parents. We'd ask 'Where's your mother?' and they'd say, 'Oh, she's working up in that place, they calls it the Enterprise Zone.' – 'Where's your father then?' – 'He's on an oil rig' – and consequently a lot of these juveniles get caught up in crime. It was sad to see it.

Charles Thomas, born 1928

They Stole My Birds

I couldn't believe it one morning when I went down to feed the pigeons. Someone had broken into the shed and fifteen birds got pinched. I think if I'd seen the people who did it then I could have shot them – I'd have had no qualms because in the pigeon world you give a lot of birds to charity, and then someone comes in and does this. Later they came back and pinched every basket I had in the shed and that really makes you think, you know – is it worth it? I had my house broken into once. I felt sick. I think they should send them to the Army – three years in the Army would do them good. I used to believe in the death penalty but in the last couple of years there's been so many appeals and people getting off it makes you think sometimes the legal system isn't right. But as regards terrorism, there should be no qualms. I think they should be shot or injected because it's premeditated, isn't it?

Graham Harris, born 1960

Crying Inconsolably

When my first husband died in Australia I brought his ashes home in a beautiful Tasmanian wood casket. I kept it in the wardrobe in my bedroom and in the summer months I was always out with the children, weather permitting. Well, this one day as soon as I opened the front door I knew something was wrong. I couldn't go in the house, something was stopping me, and I sent one of the children next door to my neighbour. She came in and as soon as I walked into the kitchen I knew

Graham Harris in his pigeon loft.

Graham's chequered pied hen Rebeca Jane, which won first prize in the Welsh Grand National pigeon race from Crieff in Scotland in 1991.

somebody had been in there. The cheeky devils had got something out of the fridge and made themselves sandwiches and left all the stuff out. We went upstairs and there was stuff all over the place. A little radio had gone and they'd broken open the casket with my husband's ashes thinking there was money or jewellery there and the ashes were all over the bed. Of course it just devastated me, it really did, and I was crying inconsolably. My next-door neighbour scooped them up and put them back in and phoned the police. They were disgusted. I took the casket down to a funeral home and they redid it for me. It really upset me.

Anne Roberts, born 1939

I Knew a Killer

Reformatories were terrible – they had a horrific effect on the children. One fellow I knew was put away for something so ridiculous it was unbelievable – petty theft or something like that. He wasn't a bad boy. When he came out he went straight to sea – in those days you did. I used to be aware of the death penalty as a child. I was frightened I'd be wrongly accused. I knew one man who killed his wife – he'd gone mental. They detained him according to the King's Pleasure. And I knew another man who supposedly killed a shopkeeper and he was put into Cardiff Prison. His daughter could actually see her father's cell from her street. He was topped but there's been a lot of doubt about his conviction.

Graham Willis, born 1935

IRA Tried to Murder Me

When I was seventeen I went into the RAF Regiment. I didn't think about killing people – it was just a job more than anything else. I was stationed in Germany and went to Holland for the weekend. Coming back in the car with two of my friends, I had my right leg shattered by terrorist gunfire, and I was also shot two or three times in my stomach. They amputated my leg in Germany. It was the IRA who did it – yes, I do regard that as a crime, definitely. They tried to murder me. In a war you know your enemies, don't you? It was an act of cowardice if anything. I wouldn't go home till I could get an artificial leg and go about on crutches – I refused to sit in a wheelchair. It was my own way of dealing with it. I'm a prosthetist now – I fit people with artificial limbs. I don't suppose I'd have gone in for this work if I hadn't lost a leg myself.

Wyn Lewis, born 1970

Matchstick Women

I think there's far too much about sex in the media. It's a natural thing but I worry about these children who are at the lower end of the academic scale. They don't want to be pushed into history and geography and maths. They should be taught how to live, how to handle money, how to care for children and how to go about seeking what you need. If they haven't got the brain power to be an academic and to go on to further education then why aren't the powers-that-be making sure they've got enough input into living skills. That's

Olwen Burton in her days as a health visitor.

Thatcher years, years of neglect, years of 'Let's all climb the ladder and not care about those behind.' We're still feeling that and drugs is a part of it. These kids believed there were no jobs and there never would be any jobs and I think the utter boredom and mediocrity of their lives drove some of them on to heavy drugs. It's just being in the wrong place at the wrong time. I think the reason heroin came here is because the Shah of Iran fell. The Ayatollah took over and they needed to make money quick and they invested in heroin and targeted Britain. I felt as if I was living in a country with a plague but nobody would admit it. Everywhere people went to get help, they came up against such stupidity. It crucified them as families.

Woman, born 1949

where it all falls down. Sex is made to seem so glamorous – when they sell a car they've got these naked women hanging over it, and these models are so thin they don't look like women. They're like matchsticks with the wood scraped off, half of them, and they're not good role models. Even people with brain power can get taken in and that's why they get involved in drugs.

Olwen Burton, born 1933

Drugs are a Plague

I think people of my age don't know anything about what young people are going through, the effects of the

A Jungle Out There

Somebody with criminal tendencies might not be a totally bad citizen because they might be caring in other ways. I'm one of those old traditional people who believe there's a bit of good in everybody and if you bring it out that's all for the better. I personally believe there's a little of the thief in every one of us. For instance, in the workplace people think they're entitled to a little perk, so if I'm an office worker I take a biro home even though that's technically stealing. I've had my car stolen on two occasions and a garage burgled once and it's not very pleasant. I don't think the majority of those who make laws realise what an impact the burglary of a dwelling house has on the occupants. We've become a softer society. We've given in to that vociferous minority who will stoop to anything to get what they want. When I was a police officer, there'd be eight to ten of us patrolling a beat in Port Talbot. We policed better then because we were much closer to the people. We weren't as accountable as a police officer is now. You used more common sense. If it was a kick up the backside or a smack across the ear that was the end of it. It worked, without a shadow of doubt. You were an omnipotent person.

John Williams, born 1939

All Hell Will Be Let Loose

It's an awful thing to say, but someone said to me the other day: 'Definition of confusion – Fathers' Day in Penrhys' [Rhondda council estate]. It's a bomb waiting to explode. You see thirteen-year-old girls out in the street and their parents don't know where they are. You'll end up with a lot of single mothers who won't disclose who the father is. If you don't know who your parents are exactly, brother will marry sister or half sister and all hell will be let loose. All the parameters are gone.

Quite a lot of the women I meet – I'm a widower – seem to feel, 'Oh, he's fair game' – the fact that they're married doesn't seem to enter into it. When they're on a night out with the girls

The strong arm of the law – Resolven section of Glamorgan regular and special constabulary, 1940.

they're after any man they can pick up, and it's very sad.

Romeo Basini, born 1937

TV Violence

Certainly society has become very violent but I'm not surprised because our films and our television are full of violence. We are fed on it day in and day out and it can be verbal as well as physical. What amazes me is that we can produce a generation of young people who are basically decent, kind and compassionate. I've been a victim of crime. I've been robbed, had my house broken into – and the person who was convicted was charged some months later with murder. I'm just lucky I wasn't in the house at the time. It's very disturbing to think somebody has been rummaging around in your wardrobes and drawers. I welcome the abolition of the death penalty because it doesn't make any kind of sense. People can repent and have a genuine change of heart and mind. The death sentence is final and there's no room for change. I think one of the best things that's happened in my lifetime is the abolition of the death penalty.

David Morris, born 1931

All That Swearing

Just think of what was on television thirty years ago and what is on now. There's a 9 o'clock watershed but at holiday time lots of ten-year-olds watch TV after that, when there's a lot of sex and violence and a huge amount of swearing going on, but they don't bat an eyelid. They're being exposed far more. There's blood and gore in *Casualty* – we never saw anything like that. I used to watch *Blue Peter* and Johnny Morris at the zoo with his funny voices. The kids would laugh at that today – they're very cynical and very demanding in their viewing.

Dr Amanda Kirby, born 1959

Mugging Unnerved Me

I was mugged just down the road a couple of months ago. I was coming out from the RAOB in Maerdy – the Buffs – and I'd only walked across the road to my car when it happened. My Buffalo regalia was stolen from me and the two boys who'd done it ran up the road. I shouted after them, 'It's no good boys, there's no money in there.' I knew that when they opened it in the back lane they'd dump it. It's unnerved me. We've gone downhill in the Valleys because if that can happen on the main road what could happen in a dark lane, or the 'gulleys' as we call them? It really hurt me, youngsters doing a thing like that. Why? There's too many loopholes in the law now. We use to respect the police … the policeman was a somebody, but there's no respect now for the police at all. Mr Hemlock was the policeman in Maerdy when I was young. He used to catch the 9 o'clock tramcar to come on night duty in Maerdy and woe betide any boys or girls who were on the streets after 9 o'clock. You could go down the side streets till your mother or father called you in but you were not allowed on the main road. You couldn't even go shopping then. He used to have a cape and he'd whop you with it. The law was there, but not nowadays. You don't even see them unless they flash past in a car.

Alfred Lawes, born 1919

Robbing Their Mates

It's getting worse – I think so, anyway. Theft more than anything, and assaults. Every Friday night you hear of someone having a hiding down in the village or somebody's house being burgled. When I was twenty-one I lived in a block of flats and I heard a rustling outside. There was a fellow living in the middle block who'd gone to rob his mate's meter and while he was out his mate was robbing his. That's what it was like then, anything for money.

Michael Crane, born 1966

Gloss Has Gone From Life

We had three of our bikes stolen during a recent family holiday. We'd gone to Bristol for a break during the October half-term and we'd taken the girls' bikes and my wife's bike as well and all three were stolen there. Our daughters wept for an hour or so. They were devastated and still can't understand why people would want to do this. Some of the gloss has gone off life for the girls and for ourselves. We've tried to explain why some people might have wanted to do this if they were poor, and explained as well about people who abuse drugs, because children of five and seven nowadays know something about that.

Alfred Lawes in his Royal Ancient Order of Buffalos regalia.

I'm not the sort of person who would say 'Hang them' but I would expect them to be fairly and justly punished if they're caught.

Dafydd Roberts, born 1956

CHAPTER 9
Conflict

RAF servicemen in the Azores in 1946. Herbert David of Cowbridge is on the extreme left, standing.

Alfred Lawes of Maerdy as a prisoner of war in Germany.

Working With Frau Muller

I was in the army and spent four years as a prisoner of war. You had to go on living and there's only one way to do that. It's no good saying, 'To hell with it', you wouldn't come home if you did that. We used to take the work in our own hands … We were working down the pit in Poland. We didn't know if we were coming up alive again, it was so bad. Sometimes we worked twelve hours down the pit and afterwards the Poles would get a certain amount of coal up. They wouldn't put posts up so the place was collapsing and you'd be dead. My mate Reg and I would make it our job to put up posts to make sure our boys were safe. We'd been two years in Munich before that but were kicked out because we were convincing the Germans they weren't winning the war. There was a big pillar with war news on it saying the British had thousands and thousands of tons of shipping sunk and so on. But scattered at the foot of the pillar were wrappers of Bournvilles chocolate and Lyons tea – we'd put them there from our Red Cross parcels. It set them thinking – if the British were so badly off, how could they be sending parcels to their prisoner of war sons – giving them stuff the Germans couldn't get themselves?

I worked in a stone yard in Munich, putting down stones to make roads. The yard was owned by Frau Muller. If she'd been a dainty dish we'd have been fighting to work for her but she had a big coat down to her ankles and a

91

headscarf and an old horse with its back bent in the middle. I said, 'I'll work with Frau Muller' and the boys all pulled my leg but I was crafty because it meant that instead of being in the same place all day I could go around Munich. I'd picked up a bit of German and one day I heard four ladies asking her if I was an Englander. She said 'No, he's from Wales – it's attached to England.' They stared at me again and said, 'Frau Muller, are they all that colour in Wales?' and she replied, 'I expect so.' Those are the things I like to remember, not the hard times.

Alfred Lawes, born 1919

IMPORTANT.   **KEEP FOR REFERENCE.**

CITY OF CARDIFF CORPORATION WATERWORKS.

HINTS TO HOUSEHOLDERS ON WATER PURIFICATION.

Read these instructions very carefully. See that you understand them and save the pamphlet for future reference in case an emergency should arise.

A. EMERGENCY SUPPLY OF DRINKING WATER

A supply of pure drinking water sufficient to tide over a short emergency of, say, two or three days, should be kept ready for use if the supply to your premises is cut off by enemy action. The water is best stored in clean stoppered bottles kept in a cool dark place.

B. POLLUTION OF THE SUPPLY.

In view of possible damage to sewers and water mains by enemy action it is advisable to take special precautions after every air raid on the City and adjoining districts within the area of supply of the Corporation. If the pressure in the water taps is normal on the morning following a raid it may be assumed that there is no risk of contamination. If possible Consumers will be warned where it is suspected that their water supply has become infected.

C. HOW TO PURIFY IMPURE WATER.

1. Boil the water for two minutes, or
2. Chlorinate the water as follows :—

   (a) Obtain a bottle of chlorinated soda solution (1% free chlorine)
   or " Milton,"
   or " Chlor-San,"
   and a small packet of photographic hypo.

   (b) Add two teaspoonfuls of chlorinated soda solution (or " Milton " or " Chlor-San ") to one 2-gallon bucket of water.

SEE OVER

When Cardiff was being blitzed in the Second World War, people were given this advice on how to help maintain a clean water supply.

All Dressed Up for a Demo

I remember going to London to protest about the local tip at Cilfynydd – this was after Aberfan. I had no concept at all about politics in that sense, how you dressed, so I went and had my hair put up in coils. I didn't have any confidence in how I dressed and my husband didn't have any idea either. He said he liked me in this and that so I wore a flowery cocktail dress with pink matching shoes and handbag and gloves – to go on a demonstration! When I look back now I'm mortified but I was so young, I didn't have a clue, but those other kids had it sussed. They were middle-class, a lot of them in college or university. I used to feel embarrassed to say I worked in a factory. I wouldn't now, I'd feel proud of it, but then I felt very unequal. So I went off to London, it was quite an exciting thing to do, but when I look back to the way I was dressed, oh dear, dear. But that's how it is with working-class people, when we're going somewhere we dress up because we spend most of our time scruffy, so let's dress up. None of the others dressed up, they were all in jeans and so I felt like a right lemon. After we got married we took part in protests about housing conditions where we were living. Then four of us women chained ourselves to the council offices and said we were going to stay there indefinitely. We thought naively that the police would come and break the chains and send us away and we would have a bit of publicity. But when the police came they said 'Good on you' and left us there. The media came and cars were going past beeping. People brought us sandwiches and the police

92

'Seven hours in a shelter … we get the raids at all times!' Harry Cullum's letter from Llandaff North, Cardiff, to his grandson Ron Cullum in Aberystwyth, 10 September 1940.

117 Tymawr Rd
Llandaff North
Cardiff
10/9/40

Dear Ron

Just a few lines in answer to your letter you said not in a Harry for a reply will me and your Gran is pretty well in Health only a bit nervy at times. 7 Hours in a Shelter at times and the banging around us we get the Raids in the day at times! but thank God we have only heard the Sharpnel up till now. I dare not tell you about whats happened in Cardiff you must guess the rest! well I hope your Dad & Mam and sisters are well. Gran wants to know why your Mam or Dad has not wrote, your Gran wrote last to them. we are both in the House on our own all the time I dont go far away only to my Allotment I got 5 Perch to pass my time away and if the Sirene goes I home for the Shelter got a bed down there

Bangor Red Cross in wartime. Mrs Hannah Rowlands is standing, second from the right.

superintendent brought us blankets from the cells. It was my first experience of solidarity. We stayed there for twenty-four hours and then went home. We realised then we had a tool we didn't have before.

I had to wrap the children up to put them to bed, it was so cold where we lived. The council wouldn't give us proper heating and they made out it was the tenants' fault, because they opened the windows and so on. One morning we occupied the council offices, we just kept on and on and on, and eventually we won, it was an amazing experience. We learned so much from that experience that we set up a South Wales Association of Tenants. We used to go round to other tenants' groups who had a problem and join in with them and say, 'Let's go round the council offices,' and we'd have sit-ins. We went to the Graig in Blaengwynfi. There were these women there, the salt of the earth, miners' wives. Their houses were running with damp, so we went down and occupied the council offices. I remember the superintendent of police coming in and saying to the leader of the group, 'Now look, Mary, if you don't move from here I'm going to have to arrest you and put you in the Black Maria and take you off.' She just looked at him and I'll never forget it, she had no teeth in, she had slippers on her feet and she said, 'Look here Dilwyn, I remember you when you was running round the Graig when there was no arse to your pants so don't tell me you've got the effing Black Maria.' It was amazing because this superintendent just crumpled in front of everybody like a little boy and

disappeared saying it was a civil matter. It's the kind of thing we did and it was a political education for me.

Jean Williams, born 1950

CHAPTER 10

Pleasure, leisure

Hannah Rowlands – second from the right – dining aboard the *Queen Mary* in August 1937.

Racing My Pigeons

Three things I really like: rugby, pigeon racing and – a very controversial subject at this time – fox hunting. The way things are, whether that will continue in the future I don't know. It's a bit bad really that townsfolk are dictating to the country folk how they should live their lives so that really does get to me sometimes. The townspeople don't really appreciate the way of life of country people. I get very bitter when you see these people protesting, as they don't really know the full facts. They're on about foxes being killed – OK, perhaps there is a certain amount of cruelty but there's nothing more cruel than taking a cow to the cattle market, selling it and sending it to the slaughterhouse. Life itself is cruel so I don't see why they moan about fox hunting.

Graham Harris, born 1960

Wild West Show

I went to a big air show Alan Cobham put on in Aberystwyth. It was 10/- [50p] a flight and I found the money somehow. We went around the National Library up Penglais, then round Penparcau and back to Blaendolau field. Only a couple of minutes it took. The pilot was sitting in the back and we were sitting in the front with a windscreen in front of us. They used to do stunts in these air shows, looping the loop and all that. I remember an air show in Aberaeron where the pilot dived down and picked up a piece of cloth from the ground with a hook under the wing.

Before that, when I was still at school, there was a huge circus in the field in Talybont, with a menagerie. They had a lot of wild animals, lions and tigers. We were living two miles away up the valley, but if you were out of doors you could hear one of the lions roaring even from there! The circus went from Talybont to Tywyn and I remember people saying a trainer was killed by a lion. My father used to tell me he went to a Wild West Show with Buffalo Bill in Aberystwyth when he was young. Annie Oakley was there too. They had about 200 horses and Indians and everything, you know. My father said they flung things up in the air and Annie Oakley would shoot them.

Dewi Evans, born 1915

Greyhound Rescue

I'm a volunteer with a charity called Greyhounds In Need, which rescues greyhounds from ill treatment in Spain. There are three or four race tracks out there and they get dogs from Ireland and England. They race them till they're totally worn out, in terrible conditions. A lady called Ann Finch runs the charity and has caused such a stir that they closed the track in Majorca. The result is that there were all these dogs in Majorca who would either be injected with washing-up liquid, hanged, or possibly tied with a brick around their neck and chucked into the sea. Anyway, I went five times to Majorca in our old beat-up van and trailer and brought out 250 dogs. I make regular trips to Spain and have rescued

500 dogs so far this year. I've always loved greyhounds, ever since I was a boy. If I saw a Spaniard hanging a dog I'd kill him.

Dai Lawrence, born 1942

Saturday Dances

There's quite a lot to do in Rhayader. There's a youth club with lots of facilities. About twenty of us just hang around in the bus shelter or the car park and if it's cold we go up to the Leisure Centre. There's a dance in Rhayader Rugby Club every Saturday and that's always a good laugh. There's a dance in Llani [Llanidloes] on a Saturday too – all sorts of music, usually hard core, drum and bass or techno.

James Price, born 1984

Outings to Barry Island

Holidays were a day at Barry Island, the nearest seaside, and you only went there through attendance at church or chapel. It was something to look forward to but hard work for me because I had to row the little ones on these boats in Cold Knap. We called at the fair on the way back, it was only a penny a ride then, but as soon as we got there my father would say, 'Oh, the train's in,' and we'd run across so we'd never have our ride. Why were we so naïve? You wouldn't get away with it today with children. I remember having new socks for Barry – tuppence [1p] a pair. There weren't a lot of new clothes. When I asked for a new frock for Easter my father used to say, 'You've got it in your belly, never mind about your back.'

Priscilla Perkins, born 1920

Dai Lawrence, dog rescuer, with some of his greyhounds in Tonteg.

Anne Roberts with her children on the beach at Barry Island in 1964. From left: Kimberley, Anthony, Karin, Anne with baby Reginald, Paul and Anne's niece Cheryl.

He Smuggled Me In!

The cinema ... a four-deep queue about 200 yards long waiting to get in. We were so poor and I was such a skinny little thing. I'd go with my brother and he would put me under his coat and the two of us would go in together until I was about seven and I got a little bit too big for that. Oh, the cinema was marvellous. We sat there and watched and it was, 'Oh, look at her complexion' and 'Look at her teeth' and she'd got it all, the heroine of the film. I'd think, 'My goodness, I hope I'll look like that when I grow up,' not realising that she'd just come out of the make-up room.

There were two cinemas in Brynamman before the war. One was the silent cinema and my father was in a group of three who played music while the films were on. He was the drummer, with a violinist and pianist. People made their own enjoyment in those days. There were spelling bees and sewing bees and knitting bees – why were they 'bees', I wonder? – things like that. Shopping was within the village and so was the entertainment.

Alethea Jones, born 1928

The Smell of Real Leather

My first recollection of anything to do with rugby was the smell of a leather rugby ball – real leather! The ball was actually bigger than I was, for I was only a little tot. They were such big rugby men in the village, they wanted me to follow in their footsteps. I learned to play in the field behind the house.

We used to play as kids on the street or on the hill. It was my father's dream that I played for Wales. It was my dream to play for Llanelli, and I fulfilled that dream. I fulfilled my father's dream as well, I'm glad to say. I can remember going to Stradey Park with my father and his coal-mining pals. They were giants to me. I was a little tot then, seven or eight years of age. They were six-footers, big men. I was with my hero – my father – and he and his friends were watching their heroes. Then their heroes became my heroes. Cliff Morgan, R.H. Williams, Bleddyn Williams, all those great names from the past, names I became aware of through my father while listening to the wireless with him and going to Stradey Park. I fell in love with the place because he had taken me there to watch this game of rugby football, the game I toyed with and played as a young boy at home. But

then seeing it being performed on this platform was wonderful, with an audience of how many thousands of people there watching the game. It really was high drama and there was a huge reality in what I saw.

Ray Gravell, born 1952

Hunting With Hounds

Saturdays I went out with the hounds at Plas Machynlleth – Colonel Beaumont's family lived there. Very posh indeed, a heck of a good family. People would follow the hounds on foot mainly in that part of the world. When I was a kid I followed the huntsman I liked, seeing what he was doing. I was a huntsman for twenty years. When the old huntsman retired they persuaded me to take over. I didn't take holidays – I

Ray Gravell, of Llanelli and Wales, in action.

didn't want anything except look after the hounds. We were breeding and taking hounds up to shows all over Wales. We had about thirty-six dogs. The hunting season begins in September and ends in March. We kill about 130 foxes in that time. Well, the foxes kill lambs all over the place so you've got to stop them, haven't you? If you didn't, what would happen to the lambs and the shepherds? That's the point, you know, and I'm sure no-one can say I'm a cruel man. All the farmers come out with guns and go around the forest. Then when the hounds put a fox up they drive it up to the guns and the fox is shot. That's how we do it and I can't see there's anything cruel about that.

Iorwerth Jones, born 1923

Chasing the Girls

I joined the Army Cadets when I was twelve. You were supposed to be fourteen but I lied about my age. I joined the band and made great mates – I still meet them today. Every summer we used to do carnivals and things that made a big impression, like the Festival of Remembrance in Guildhall in Swansea. Then we had a Remembrance

Harry Cullum – the runner on the right – narrowly lost to J. Ferguson in the 600 yards world championship race at Dundee football ground on 30 September 1901.

Ron Cullum breasts the tape to win a half-mile event in Aberystwyth.

Parade and I played the *Last Post* once on my own on the promenade in Swansea. I was bugler, then I went to tenor drums and then side drums. My sister taught me to jive when I was little and I used to go to dances with my mates. We'd go to cadets, then on the weekend we'd go to the Embassy dances, chasing all the girls.

Terry Stewart, born 1943

Grandad, the Champion Runner

My grandfather Harry Cullum was a champion runner round about the turn of the century. He won the Welsh half-mile and quarter-mile championships and was also the Welsh senior cross-country champion. He turned professional in 1898 and became the world half-mile champion. I

remember winning the half-mile race at Ardwyn school and one of the teachers, George Rowlands, saying, 'Well done, Ronnie, you'll be like your grandfather!' I was about thirteen then. I'd grown up knowing about him, of course, and when I visited him in Cardiff in the war I found out he had all these programmes of his running days and all this history came out. I said, 'Why can't I look after all this for you in case a few bombs come along here?' He didn't want to part with them but the following year I went back to Cardiff and coaxed him into letting me bring them home and that winter I patched them all up. When I went in the Army I ran for HQ Southern Command in the *News of the World* road relay in Mitcham in 1943. My grandfather never saw me run but he gave me advice. Relaxation was the key word – relaxation while you run. If you're really tense you get tied up and that's no good at all. He was a friendly sort of chap – there was plenty of laughter with him. He became commissionaire at the Co-operative Wholesale Society in Cardiff and had his own vegetable garden when he retired.

I liked football as well as running and played for Aberystwyth Town just after the war, in the side captained by Ted Bevan. One of our biggest matches was against Barry Town in the Welsh Senior Cup – there was a tremendous gate for Aber, well over 3,000. I had the job of marking the old Arsenal and Wales player, Les Jones. We lost 2-1 but I remember hitting the bar with two minutes to go! I also played for Rovers, a local team started by Victor Williams and Caradog Fisher Davies. We played

football as it should be played – on the ground. It was great fun.

Ron Cullum, born 1925

Dad Played for Wales

My father William O'Neill was a great rugby forward in his day. They often called him Neill not O'Neill – I don't know why. He made 204 appearances for Cardiff and won 11 Welsh caps. He was in the Welsh team that beat England 22-0 at Swansea in 1907. One of the newspaper cuttings I've kept says he was 'magnificent in the line-out and one of the best forwards the Cardiff club ever possessed.' His son Garry – my brother – was also a fine

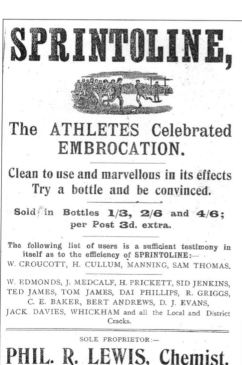

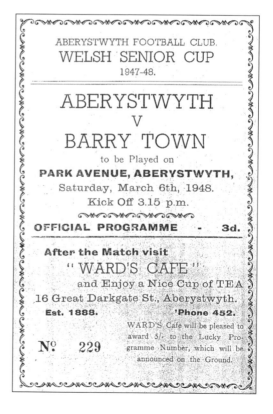

Aberystwyth Rovers' championship-winning team, 1949/50. Skipper Ron Cullum has the ball at his feet. Club founder Vic Williams is on the extreme left, back row.

player. He captained St Peter's team in Cardiff in 1924/25. He played for Cardiff in 1929/30 but had a serious illness and never played after the age of eighteen. He died when he was twenty-one.

William (Bill) O'Neill, born 1908

We wuz Robbed!

My brother and I sang a lot in the Urdd Eisteddfod when we were growing up. I'm not Welsh-speaking but I can understand a little and I can sing it and read it. We used to sing a duet and that's what launched our passion for music. My brother was fourteen when we recorded our first single and we were very popular in Wales, especially with the young girls. We managed to get to the semi-finals at the Urdd Eisteddfod and we came on and sang a duet and all the girls started screaming, but they disqualified us because they said it wasn't in the tradition of the Eisteddfod! We were very influenced by the Beatles and the Everly Brothers. We were the best there too!

Revd Ray Bevan, born 1950

City Allotments

Before the war my father had a great interest in gardening and there was a lot of competition from neighbours. If your garden came up to scratch you were the talk of the town. If your garden wasn't right they'd say, 'If his garden's

St Thomas Community Centre cricket team, Swansea, early 1950s. Skipper Harold Wilson is seated in the centre of the middle row. Charles Henry Thomas – father of Charles Thomas, later Lord Mayor of Swansea – is second from the left in the middle row.

like that imagine what his house is like.' That was the mentality of it. They all shared their plants and had allotments just behind their houses in Tremorfa. If you wanted to keep a few pigs or chickens you could do that. Every Sunday we would dig up the veg for a week, load up our little truck with wheels on and push it back. It was very countryfied.

Graham Willis, born 1935

CHAPTER 11

Life and death

A patient at the South Wales Sanatorium, Talgarth, 1949/50.

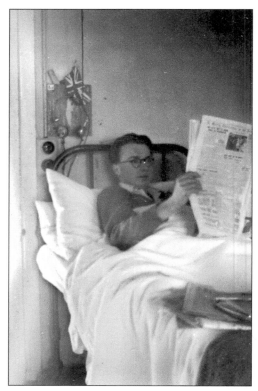

Patients at the South Wales Sanatorium, Talgarth, 1949/50.

Goose Grease

My mother used to give me cod liver oil and malt out of a big jar with a big spoon and I hated it. It was like putting thick treacle in your mouth and it made me heave. My brother Jack was very crafty, because he'd say, 'Give it to Charlie, he's smaller than me and needs it more' and I'd be kicking him under the table. Then there was syrup of figs to make you go to the toilet, worm cakes and Andrew's Liver Salts every Saturday night, and if you had a bad chest they'd rub goose grease all over it.

Charles Thomas, born 1928

Scourge of Mankind

In 1960 when I was carrying one of the children I was told I had TB. It was a big shock because when I was a child a friend of mine had it and she was shut away in a hospital. We were led to believe that TB was something awful, you stayed away from it, it was dirty, only dirty people had it, so when I had it I felt dirty. I had to go into hospital and we were grumbling one morning about the toast, one said it was burnt and the other said this and that, and a small nurse came in – she was only about five foot – and said, 'Ladies, a year ago you would all have been dying.' They'd brought out this new cure for tuberculosis and we were some of the first ones to have it. We were given tablets. I think it's wonderful that they could cure tuberculosis, which had been a scourge of mankind.

Alethea Jones, born 1928

TB Taboo

My father ran away to sea during the war and was torpedoed so his attitude to life was not like everybody else's. He wasn't worried about academic success, life was a bit of an adventure, you had to go for it when you could. He'd had TB and couldn't get work. TB was like Aids, nobody wanted to employ you if you'd had it.

Jenny Edwards, born 1953

Kill or Cure

I had a bad attack of flu in May 1948, when I was fifteen. I began spitting blood and they found I had TB. I was nursed at home by my mother for five months and then went into Talgarth Sanatorium. It was kill or cure in those days – the windows were always wide open and in winter the snow would blow into the ward. I was afraid I might die like my brother before me but I gradually got better. It was the old regime of fresh air and bedrest – plenty of it – just before they brought in drugs like streptomycin which revolutionised treatment. My right lung was collapsed by pumping air through the pleural walls. It was only much later that I discovered how dangerous this was – we were told nothing in those days. Our

bodies weren't our own – they belonged to the doctors. But I'm grateful for the treatment because without it I'd probably have died. Talgarth was a real education. The patients came from all walks of life and it was a rough introduction to the world for someone like me. You grew up quickly there and – if my experience was typical – you were changed fundamentally as a result. I was in there for exactly two years and was still being refused life insurance four or five years after my discharge.

Herbert Williams, born 1933

Held Down By My Brothers

We had a very poor diet in the '50s and I used to suffer a lot of boils. We had a big wooden kitchen table and a coal fire and I can remember my brothers holding me down and my father squeezing the boils to get the pus out and my mother making kaolin poultices looking like grey putty. She put the kaolin in a saucepan of boiling water to soften and then smeared it on a piece of lint, and while it was still hot they'd put it on and break the boils.

Terry Stewart, born 1943

Mum's Will To Live

My Mum died of cancer when I was twenty-seven. She died twelve weeks after my wedding – I was the last of her three daughters to be married. I'm convinced she thought, 'That's it, they're all married, I can do my own thing now,' so to speak. I know that's a funny thing to say, but she had such a strong will to live. Our family changed substantially after her death. They always say mums and daughters stay friends after you grow up, don't they? We would go shopping and do things together. It's something we've missed. She was very pivotal in our growing up. She was so constructive about death. She actually wrote us a letter saying things like, 'I've trained Dad to manage the ironing.' She was absolutely incredible. She really had it sorted.

Louise Prynne, born 1958

All Down to a Virus!

When I was a child it was always, 'Keep your vest tucked in your knickers to keep your back covered' or, 'put your gloves and hat on or you'll get cold,' things like that. We're less aware of prevention now it's, 'We'll take an antibiotic and get rid of it.' And you've got all these viruses now. You go to the doctor and they say 'Oh, it's a virus.' Christ knows, if you went there pregnant they'd say 'Oh, that's a virus!'

Jenny Edwards, born 1953

Five Heart Bypasses

I should have died in 1990 but thank God I was spared. I had a massive heart attack and it bloody hurt, I can tell you. I woke up on a trolley in a tunnel, all pipes and cobwebs and God knows what, and there's a nurse pushing me and another nurse alongside me, and the first thing that went through my

head was, they're taking me to the morgue. I looked up at the nurse and said, 'I'm not dead, love' and she said 'I hope you're not or I'll get bloody sacked.' They were taking me to one of the coronary units through a tunnel underground. I often see that nurse, she lives down the road, and she says, 'Are you dead yet?' and I say, 'No, not yet.' I've had two more heart attacks since and five heart by-passes.

Dai Lawrence, born 1942

Grieving Takes Years

At one time the coffin would be kept in the home until the burial. Nowadays there's a tendency to put people in the chapel of rest. The funeral ceremony has changed too. If someone has a favourite pop song it's played. We have a different attitude to death but I don't think we come to terms with it now in the best manner. As soon as the funeral is over people are left to their own devices but grieving takes many months and years and that's the way it ought to be.

John Williams, born 1939

My Pal Glanville

My bosom pal Glanville was killed by a lorry just as war was declared. I was devastated. It meant I had no pal at all and it must have taken two years before I had another. That was a miner's son everyone called Arthur Bach and we've been pals from that day to this. Glanville's death hit me very hard. I

Serving Christmas dinner at the C&A Hospital, Bangor. Dr Gareth Hughes is wielding the carving knife.

remember to this day him lying in his coffin, strangely enough with his hair unnaturally parted in the middle and rouge on his cheeks. I was asked by my Auntie Bronnie would I like to take a look at him and I felt too ashamed to say no. One didn't want to be thought of as being nervous but I was nervous of course and still am.

David Morris, born 1931

They Wouldn't Let Me See Her

My mother died on my tenth birthday, that's one of the worst memories I have. She had a knock on the head and it caused a tumour on the brain and it killed her. She went a bit silly really, some people would say mental. In those days they didn't have the technology they've got now. She used to see things that weren't there, it was all part and parcel of the tumour. The day she died, I'd gone to the pictures – the old Coliseum cinema in Canton [Cardiff]. It was the school holidays and because it was my birthday I went to the matinee with my friends. I was playing in the street after when a couple of kids came up to me and said, 'Ha ha, your mother's dead.' I started shouting and screaming and battered the two of them and ran in the house screaming, and that's how I found out it was true. If I'd gone straight in instead of playing in the street I'd have been told properly. We weren't allowed to go to the funeral. Young children didn't go to funerals in those days. They wouldn't let me see her. They thought it would be too traumatic for me. She was tall, well built, a very good mother.

Anne Roberts, born 1939

Dad Was My Hero

My father was my hero. He was a giant of a man. We were more like two friends together or two brothers. The bond was seemingly unbreakable but it had to break, unfortunately. He'd had this very bad back injury underground and it had curtailed his activities. He was in plaster from his neck to his midriff for nine months, but he would still go for a walk on the mountain and I would go with him. He was renowned throughout the valley for his strength but he had lost his physical prowess and that had a huge effect on him psychologically. Looking back, I remember him in bed crying, and that to me was very strange. I was thirteen years of age and to see my hero crying because he was in pain with his back did shock me.

One day – I was fourteen by then – he failed to come back from a walk on the mountain. Night came and my mother became very agitated, so I decided to go and get two neighbours, Dai and John. I told them my father had been gone since the morning and hadn't come back, so the three of us set off to look for him. I didn't have a torch but they had torches. I made a bit of a spurt and ran on ahead in the darkness through the bushes, and something took me to the spot where he was. The dog had never left his side. It was total darkness but I fell on my knees. I knew then that was it. From then on that night is a bit of a blur. I came back and couldn't tell my mother. I begged Dai

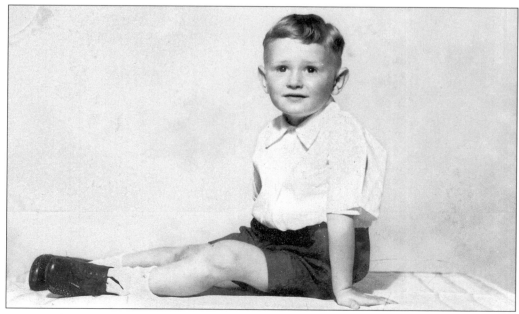

Ray Gravell as a boy.

and John not to take me back to the house until she knew. I couldn't face her. He'd shot himself twice. There was no explanation. He left no note. It was the seventh of January 1966 – a Saturday. What torments he had been going through in his mind leading up to that one can only imagine.

My mother was a very attractive lady. She was forty-three years of age and she never went with another man, she just stayed here in the house and never went out socially for a drink or to the pictures with a member of the opposite sex. She never had a relationship after my father died. It was a relief when his body came back to the house. I wanted to see him and they relented in the end. They took off the coffin lid and as I looked at his face, it wasn't him. It was my father, it was his body, but he wasn't there, and a huge relief came over me. I remember something that happened when he was still alive. I was lying in bed and it hit me that one day I would die. I was scared and woke my father and mother up. They said, 'Oh, jump in here' and I felt safe with them.

Ray Gravell, born 1952

Dealing With Death

When I was a newly-qualified young doctor, one Christmas Day a man was rushed into hospital – he was about forty-five. We tried to resuscitate him but couldn't and I, as a houseman – the lowliest of the low – had to go and tell his wife and two teenage children that he had died. I walked down the corridor after and just cried. Nobody counselled and supported me. I had to go to the

Ray Gravell's hero – his father.

ward and get on with the next job and I think that was terribly hard. You were still very young to deal with death in that way. It was all very raw.

Dr Amanda Kirby, born 1959

CHAPTER 12
Getting older

A sight for sore eyes, whatever age you are – one of the last electric trains on the historic Mumbles Railway in Swansea.

Charlotte Williams and her granddaughter, Ruby Honey, aged five months.

New Lease of Life

I've got a friend who retired fifteen years ago – he was a headmaster, and I don't think he ever enjoyed it. But since his retirement he's blossomed because he's following his hobbies. He's beekeeping and doing community work and acting or whatever. But if work is the only thing in your life then you've lost your role when you stop.

Gwen Hughes, born 1933

Growing Older

You've got to accept it – growing older. I'm still twenty-one as far as my brain is concerned. The body's a bit knackered but the rest of me's OK!

Dai Lawrence, born 1942

If I Won the Lottery …

My mother's in a nursing home and how she's alive nobody knows because she's hung on for six months, a little shadow. I see her every day and people think I'm silly and that I visit her too much, but she's wonderful and I don't know another lady like her and that's the honest truth. I had her at home here for two and a half years and we realised she had this horrible bone-crumbling disease, osteoperosis. It's hideous. If she bent down to pick something up her ribs would break. She needed care and unfortunately she needed more than I could give her. If I won the Lottery she'd be home in a taxi and I'd have nurses round the clock. I wouldn't leave her there, no.

Sally Pryce, born 1945

Archive of Ancestry

Last year my father died and my granddaughter was born so suddenly I switched a whole generation. That focussed my mind on growing older, and growing older as a black person in a very isolated environment for black people. It's one of my issues. My granddaughter is blue-eyed and fair-haired and my father dies a black man and you feel your blackness is washing away as he goes. He's an archive of that ancestry and it goes away with him, and you look at your granddaughter and you think, 'Well, what can I pass on to her of that?' because it's not going to be visible to her in the way it was visible to me.

Charlotte Williams, born 1954

Keeping Me Young

We live thankfully in a society where you're as old as you feel and that's tremendous. My parents were almost middle-aged before I was out of napkins. I have a relationship with my own children and with my grandchildren which is second to none. They treat me almost as an equal and I think that keeps you young. I've always kept fit. I'm sixty years of age but I feel a lot younger. I think physical fitness

Jersey Park pensioners in Swansea dressed up to kill for a day out in the 1930s. Jack Thomas is the mischievous boy perched on the railings.

114

helps mental fitness. If you say you're growing old you just curl up in the corner.

John Williams, born 1939

Old Age Starts at Eighty

Years ago I used to think the retiring age of sixty to sixty-five was old, but not now . If you hear someone has died at sixty five you say, 'Good God that's young.' My mother was seventy last week and she's pretty sprightly. When you think of old today, you're talking eighty. My wife reckons it's a man's world, but I go around a lot of sheltered dwellings with my work and you don't see many men – they've passed on. I'd never put my parents in a home. You hear so much on TV about abuse in those homes. I've got real doubts about some of them.

Graham Harris, born 1960

Whisky Kept Nana Going

Nana – my mother's mother – was ninety-nine when she died. She was bedridden for years but she loved a drop of whisky. Towards the end she didn't know who half the people were but so long as you showed her the bottle of whisky you were the best thing since sliced bread. 'Oh, my darling, you've brought me my medicine!' The doctors used to say it was this that kept her going so long.

Anne Roberts, born 1939

When Your Parents Go ...

Fifty is a landmark because afterwards bits of your body start to go wrong, though it doesn't mean you have to feel old. I had breast cancer which I think I've survived and I feel better than before but it brings home your mortality, which is not a bad thing. My mother was eighty-one when she died. She'd had a stroke and to be absolutely honest she had very little quality of life at that time, but you never want your mother not to be there. When your parents go from the top of the ladder you're not a daughter any more and it's quite hard. When Mam died I helped the nurse to wash her and that was very important. I don't know why, I can't say I enjoyed it, but it helped me enormously to come to terms with it.

Mair McGeever, born 1940

I Won't Stop at Sixty-five

It doesn't frighten me. I'm pretty healthy, touch wood. My grandmother lived to a grand old age – ninety-two, I think she was. You can still have fun even when you're old. There's nothing stopping you. If I'm still fit enough I'll work, that's how I look at it. I won't stop when I'm sixty-five. A good old age now I would say is mid-eighties or nineties. If I didn't live to that age I'd be disappointed.

Michael Crane, born 1966

As the song has it, 'Were there ever such devoted sisters?' The Misses Hughes of Ty Isa, Glan Conwy, early this century. Maggie and Sue are standing, and Gwen, Sally, Fanny and Kit sitting.

Lloyd George's Daughter

My grandmother who lived here [in Cricieth] died at the age of ninety-seven with a stroke. She was David Lloyd George's daughter and she had married from No. 10 Downing Street – she was quite a character. She outlived most of her friends but her last few years were sad. She used to be quite miserable about things and she was making it worse for herself. You would come and visit her and have nothing but complaints, and as a teenager you would rebel against this. Yet you know you'll be there yourself one day and you hope

you won't be a miserable person too. And then I have another grandmother living in Anglesey who is very independent, lives in her own house and is refusing to move out. I admire her so much. She never complains and she's worked so hard all her life as a farmer's wife. She's so proud of her children, so proud of her grandchildren and she's enjoyed life to the full, and to me that's great. So you've got one woman who had it all, met so many wonderful people, went to every important event and lived a life that probably many people envied. Then you had my other grandmother who worked so hard, nothing came easy, and yet she in her late years is so happy with life. It make you think, doesn't it?

Davina Carey-Evans, born 1965

You're Never Safe Again

As you get older you get more fearful of things because you've experienced life and you see more dangers. You always worry, especially when you have children – you worry for them. That alters your life, you're never safe ever again, are you? Because there's a bit of you out there doing things that you can't control. You never grow out of that, indeed no. It's in the job description.

Jenny Edwards, born 1953

I Want to Live to be 100

My Mum is forty-one and my Dad's forty. Old is thirty-nine so Mum and Dad are old. My Nan is seventy something. I want to live to be 100 at least.

Daisy Evans, born 1990

Four generations: Annie Hughes, her son Robert Hughes behind her, her granddaughter Ann Roberts and her great-grandchildren Sian and Gareth.

CHAPTER 13
Beliefs

Mrs Hannah
Rowlands with the
clock presented to her
by Beulah
Congregational
Chapel, Bangor, for
her twenty-five years'
work organising the
preachers' rota.

Curing the Bewitched

There used to be superstitions in the old days. I remember old Lottie living down there – she believed in those things, you know. Duw, aye … and in witches, you know. They used to believe in them in the old days, you see. And there was an old fellow in Ponterwyd who used to cure people – only fraud, he was. Ned the Conjuror, we called him – he cured the bewitched. There was an old fellow in Goginan, John Athan his name was, and he could cure a wound, I don't know how. He cured my sister. She burnt her leg on the motor-cycle – I had an old bike with the pipes up and she was on the back and she burnt her leg and couldn't cure it. She went to Jack Athan and he cured her straight away, I don't know how he did it but it's quite true, he did it – yet I don't believe in it. And there was a barber in Aberystwyth, Tom Jones the Barber – he cut somebody with a razor and Ned cured it straight away. Whether it's true or not … it's difficult to believe that, I don't know …

Dewi Evans, born 1915

'New Age' Jesus

I think there has to be an almighty power somewhere and I'm certain there was a bloke called Jesus Christ who was incredible. If he was about today he would be a New Age traveller and everybody would be listening and saying what a good bloke he was, without being unkind to him as they were years ago. But as for a faith … I don't know I have one any more, though I went to church every Sunday until six years ago.

Sally Pryce, born 1945

Chapel-going Habit

We go to chapel but I think that's the least important thing in religion, really. A lot of it is part of the Welsh culture and it's a habit, though it's a good habit and I enjoy it. I'd like to think that I try to follow Christ's example although it's difficult, isn't it?

Gwen Hughes, born 1933

Praying for Everyone

I pray every night before I close my eyes and my wife does the same. I pray for my family that have gone and my present family, and believe it or not I always pray for the heads of state. I pray for the Prime Minister, irrespective of who it is. I'm a Labour man, but I even prayed for Margaret Thatcher. My Christian belief is not only to pray for myself and friends but to pray for our enemies, and be ready to forgive.

Charles Thomas, born 1928

Charlotte Williams at her graduation day in Bangor University.

Magic and Myth

I don't associate with any church or following or sect or anything like that. My mother was Bible-black as they say, so she quoted from the Bible which was very central to her, but I haven't felt the need for that kind of collective religious observation. I'm happy with the idea of a higher being but honestly, so far as faith is concerned I don't think everything has been proved. I think it's something to do with being in Africa as a child that allows you to accept the magical, the mythical, the extraordinary. You don't feel the need to challenge it or have it proved to you scientifically. I love myth and I love the idea of things happening magically. I thank my lucky stars and I pray sometimes. I'd be quite happy to join in other people's prayers and in fact I've done that. I find things like those Druids at the Eisteddfod very scary. I don't really go in for that. I think it's been quite oppressive to a lot of people.

Charlotte Williams, born 1954

C of E Agnostic

I mostly go to church on Sunday. My father was churchwarden and also an atheist. He belonged to the Rationalist Press Association. He supported the idea of the Church as a social institution supplying a lot of social needs. A friend of mine calls himself a C of E agnostic – I think there are many. I'm also a non-believer but I do believe in the Church of England and I don't think that's hypocritical. I don't feel any conflict there as I feel it's been at the core of our liberty of belief in this country. It's protected people.

Lord Raglan, born 1927

Stepping Out of Line

I was seventeen when I was called up in 1944 and I declared myself a conscientious objector on good Christian and political grounds. The men were great in work but the people who came back from the war were officers and the working-class officer class was the worst of the lot. They made my life very miserable. I remember that when I'd had my calling-up papers my schoolmate Spencer Thomas was behind me. The man said, 'What do you want to be?' and I replied 'CO please.' Spencer said, 'You want to be a commanding officer?' so I said, 'No, conscientious objector.' I was taken behind the counter into a little room where the employment exchange officers were trying to persuade me to change my mind, but I didn't. I had three tribunals in Cardiff before a High Court judge who recognised I was quite genuine. I was put to work in a pit for a year with 400 Poles in Pontypridd, then I went back to the foundry in Llanelli and tried for a scholarship with Ruskin College, Oxford. I was fortunate enough to get a trade union scholarship of £80 a year and then they gave me a State scholarship. I went to Ruskin for two years, came back to Swansea to do my diploma in social work and youth work, and then went to university in Aberystwyth.

David Morris, born 1931

Pretending to Pray

My Nan is still religious, still Roman Catholic and goes to church every week. My Mum took us to church until we were toddlers and then I think she just fell by the wayside and dropped out of it. I've never felt religious. When I was little I tried to copy my Nan because she shared the same bedroom and every night she used to kneel against the bed and whisper her prayers. She had these little prayer cards and I always remember sitting on my bed and

Nativity play in Capel Siloh, Caernarfon, 1953.

asking her for the cards. I couldn't do it as fast as she could and I used to make lip-smacking noises as if I was praying. No, I don't believe in God. I believe in morality if you like. We all have a duty to be kind to one another, to make sure your fellow man is comfortable and that you don't behave badly towards others and I think that's enough. I always had a lot of arguments with a friend at school who was a born again Christian. I used to argue that if I gave up a bus seat to an old lady that says a lot more than kneeling in church every Sunday and telling somebody that he's greater than me. If there's a God he doesn't want to hear that. Why would he want us telling him how wonderful he is? I think he would be very egotistical if that was the case.

Elizabeth Smith, born 1971

Is Anyone There?

When my father died I still believed in God. People said he'd gone to join his Saviour and I believed all that because he was very religious. Then I lost my faith and I found my mother's funeral very hard. For me it's unimaginable to think there's a God who cares, who is jealous and who can prevent things happening. I can understand the spirituality of it all but I can't understand to whom you can pray to say please help me at a certain time, because I don't believe there's anybody there who can respond to that.

Mair McGeever, born 1940

They're Kidding Themselves

My mother and father go to chapel. I was dragged along as a child and I stopped going when they stopped dragging me along. I find it very strange, if there is a God, that so many atrocious things have happened. People who believe in him always have an answer. It's like he can do anything but he only does it for a reason and I feel sometimes they're kidding themselves.

Wyn Lewis, born 1970

I Still Go to Chapel

Annwyl, yes, we had to go to chapel and I still go. I've never stopped and I never will. I believe in God, yes. When we were kids we had to go to chapel in the morning, back here for dinner, back then at 2 o'clock for Sunday school and then chapel again in the evening. Tired after Saturday, isn't it – you would like to be in bed all day Sunday but had no chance, they were keen, you know. Everybody was at that time and the chapel was full.

Iorwerth Jones, born 1923

It Changed My Life

I was in a rock band for five or six years and went to see a film called The Greatest Story Ever Told, about the life of Christ, and it had an incredible effect on my life insomuch that I saw the light. I got converted or whatever you want to call it. It was a transforming experience, bang! It changed my life. There were lots of things happening but when I said 'God, I give you my life' it was an instant thing and from then on the change was remarkable. My mother used to send me to Sardis Sunday School just to get rid of me for an hour. She thought we were there but we ended up going up the woods or something like that. But there were times when we did go to Sunday school and I remember the old flannelgraphs – telling Bible stories using little felt stick-ons. Sometimes the donkey would fall on the floor or the tree would be upside-down, but it must have planted some seed in there because the only 'O' level I passed was in religious education, as I was fascinated with the person of Moses. I thought he was Charlton Heston for a long time. So although there was no conscious effort on my parents' part to put any religious influence in me I think Sardis Sunday School did have an effect.

Revd Ray Bevan, born 1950

I Just Don't Know

I go to church when I go to my Nan's house because she always goes. I'm not sure if I believe in God because it's hard, you just don't know. It's the same with Santa, and it's funny with Santa because it's always the adults who've seen him. God could be a complete make up.

Daisy Evans, born 1990

CHAPTER 14
The millennium and beyond

Young Louise Prynne blowing away the
hours in her childhood.

Say Twenty Hundred!

Why do they keep talking about 'The year two thousand' when it's twenty hundred? We say nineteen hundred and eighteen hundred so why not say twenty hundred? I think we've all been so excessively smug, going on about the Millennium and then this Kosovo comes along, to prove we haven't gone so far forward after all. I think the Millenium's a lot of media hype, I really do.

Jenny Edwards, born 1953

Just Another Day

No, I won't be celebrating the Millennium. It's just another day, isn't it? To me it's nothing special. What I'd like to do is come back – not for long – in a hundred years' time just to see how much further the world has progressed by then. If you think how things have changed in the past century, it's incredible.

Dai Lawrence, born 1942

Fantastic Youth

I think we would be a wise and civilised nation if we were conscious of what we want to take forward. We might have the capability to do something but decide that isn't progress, and making those decisions is my sense of what progress is. We've seen that in terms of nuclear armaments and nuclear waste and in cloning. I think as a society we could be more progressive about things like euthanasia, giving people choices over the timing of their own death. I'm an optimistic person. I think there are hopeful signs that Britain is more willing to accept diversity and differences and mainstream that idea. This intermixing as well as people having distinctive ethnic traditions and cultures is part and parcel of Britishness now and it's nice. The young people today are fantastic – they're very resilient and adaptable and interesting ideas are coming from them. They're more reflective about their attitudes and the issues of society than I ever was.

Charlotte Williams, born 1954

Culling the Old

I don't think there'll be so many people alive after the age of seventy in a hundred years' time. You won't see people in nursing homes as you do today. Hopefully they'll have cured a lot of illnesses but something else will have come along to take people away, it's nature's culling. When I say people won't last beyond seventy … I think healthy people will but for the others, I honestly think euthanasia is the best way. Though how I'll feel when they come with the injection and say 'It's your turn today' I don't know. I'm being flippant now but I don't want to be like my Mum, no …

Sally Pryce, born 1945

We're No Wiser

What's next? There's no future for me, I'm ninety. I hope I'll see the Millennium but I don't know what it will be like except there will three noughts instead of three nines. I don't think there's any other difference, do you? But seriously, it's frightening because of these bombs they are making, this nuclear business. People are not getting any wiser, look how they are in the Balkans now. They can't live together.

Hannah Rowlands, born 1909

Parents at Home

The balance between home and work has to change. It's not really about women's independence but about the balance being right. I think we've gone too far with everybody going out to work and nobody being home … I look forward to more flexible working so there can be parents around more for kids. There's no doubt about it, you don't get enough quality time with your kids. As a parent and a working mother, I think juggling is the most difficult thing to do and I hope the balance will be better in the next fifteen years.

Dr Amanda Kirby, born 1959

Save Our Villages

Several large estates have developed in Aberporth since the 1970s on land which I remember as fields. A sentimental reaction is to feel sad about this. You can understand why people want to retire to places like Aberporth because it's so beautiful there and these houses are needed for these people, I suppose. But I do feel there are times when we could look at the existing housing stock in villages and think about converting or adapting those houses in some way so that people can live in existing nineteenth-century houses. I think it would help to conserve our towns and villages.

Dafydd Roberts, born 1956

Harri Hughes with his dad's new car in 1959. What will inventions of the future be like?

Youth having its fling – nine-year-old Daisy Evans, on the brink of the Millennium.

Back to the Land

Assuming we can fight off the developers and the vandals, who are a real curse, and the fly tippers, we hope to have more people taking up allotments in Cardiff. If you have the sort of job that isn't too physically taxing you need a hobby and although it seems mundane, gardening can be an excellent hobby and I think we can attract young people. Our area in Cardiff is flat and might be suffering more from flooding, possibly, because of global warming. The seasons are no longer the seasons we grew up with. Everything has shifted around a bit. I think people are going to have to start moving to the higher ground. That's on the cards.

Graham Willis, born 1935

Good Times Ahead

When people complain, I keep thinking … I was born in 1940 in the middle of a war. My parents were expecting the Germans to invade us. It must have been a dreadful time. We are much better off now than they were then. I'm very optimistic. I think it's going to be wonderful. Very idealistically, I'd like to think that people will embrace all cultures and everything, not to feel they are better or worse than anybody else.

Mair McGeever, born 1940

Dawn of a New Era

I tended to say it's just another day and another year but I feel now that people have the sense that there's going to be the dawn of a new era, a new beginning. I hope the politicians will start looking at the real issues because I think that 90% of people are law-abiding and only want to live peaceful lives, but they aren't allowed to do so, unfortunately.

John Williams, born 1939

Symbolic

The Millennium is obviously a symbolic point for a lot of people, so it's as important as they will make it.

Nerys Patterson, born 1943

Time Won't Stand Still

We're going to have very big fireworks in our field. We don't own any animals in the field so it's all right. I used to have a rabbit and a dog but the dog savaged the rabbit and sheep so it had to go. I'm going to do my grade one in piano and violin and harp but I don't believe there are going to be those tall ugly buildings and cars flying all round the place, I definitely don't think that's going to happen. There'll be some new inventions because you can't go through about fifteen years without inventing anything, can you?

Daisy Evans, born 1990